PAT[...]
PAIN-F[...]

D0000813

Arthritis is the nation's number-one crippling disease, but there are now very effective methods of treatment that improve the overall health of arthritis sufferers. THE ARTHRITIS HANDBOOK introduces these methods into your home. It will answer your questions; it will answer your needs.

"This handbook will be of great use to patients with arthritis, and to those interested in reading about it because someone in the family is affected. The book is extremely factual and highly informative."

L. H. Calabrese, D.O., F.A.C.P.
Head, Section of Clinical Immunology
The Cleveland Clinic Foundation

"What the authors say is true: physicians often do not provide their patients with enough information. THE ARTHRITIS HANDBOOK serves its audience well."

John Baum, M.D.
Director, Arthritis and Clinical
Immunology Unit
Monroe Community Hospital
University of Rochester
School of Medicine and Dentistry

THE ARTHRITIS HANDBOOK

Theodore W. Rooney, D.O.
Patty Ryan Rooney

BALLANTINE BOOKS • NEW YORK

Library of Congress Catalog Card Number: 84-73462

ISBN 0-345-33561-9

This edition published by arrangement with Wm. C. Brown Company, Publishers

Manufactured in the United States of America

First Ballantine Books Edition: September 1986

Contents

ಸಿಸಿಸಿ

v

Foreword

The Arthritis Handbook was written for people who happen to have arthritis. It contains everything you wanted to know about arthritis, and you didn't even ask. It was written by a physician to ensure that the facts are straight, and it was written by a writer so that the facts would be understandable and (we hope) more interesting.

The Arthritis Handbook contains information and ideas to help you gain control over arthritis. You may have never thought about arthritis as something you control, but this book will show you how.

You probably already know something about arthritis, its types and treatments. But you may not realize that it is possible to achieve a high degree of health even if you have arthritis. There is a spectrum of health within any chronic disease, especially arthritis. To achieve the highest degree of health of which you are capable, there are some things you should know and do.

We think of health mostly in terms of the absence of illness, and that is partly true. You have arthritis, but that does not mean that you will never be healthy again. If you take good care of yourself—and that means exercising, getting plenty of rest, eating well, and taking medication to help your arthritis—it is quite possible that you will be healthier than those people who don't have arthritis but neglect to take good care of themselves.

Good health also includes good mental health, and good mental health may be even more important for the person who has arthritis. Mind and body are one, and attitude plays a very important role in how you feel physically. Your attitude begins with knowing about arthritis and then using that knowledge to help you control your arthritis.

Attitude comes from within and cannot be taught. However, the Arthritis Handbook suggests many guidelines to get you started.

Because one of the persons responsible for this book is a writer, this book begins with a story...

Acknowledgments

To Kelly, Maggie, and Jacy, for trying very hard to understand that writing is work.

To my mother, Evelyn Ryan, who is so much a part of me and my writing.

To my father, the late Clark Ryan, who is surely smiling at this moment.

To my mother and father, Edward and Marilyn Rooney, for their support, emotionally and financially, in my medical career.

To Karen Thomas, M.A., Exercise Physiologist, Mercy Pain Center, for providing the exercises used.

To Rob McClain, M.D., illustrator extraordinaire, for medical and exercise illustrations.

To Betsy Schoeller, R.D., and Kim Rehm, R.D., Clinical dietitians, Mercy Hospital Medical Center, for providing excellent menus and recipes for eating well.

To Sue Debe and Martha Cushion, for typing and retyping and retyping...

To the Health Education Dept., Mercy Medical Center, and especially to Mary Kay Casey and Marlo Rold for support, encouragement, and ideas.

To the Iowa Chapter of the Arthritis Foundation, for providing facts and statistics.

1 A Story: The Last Thing on My Mind

ॐॐॐॐ

I knew all about arthritis. I had heard about it for years from various family members. In fact, at our annual reunions, the conversation would invariably come around to arthritis. One relative in particular would consistently catch me in a corner and talk my ear off about her arthritis intrusion. She would carry on and on about her stiff and swollen joints, perpetual fatigue, and describe the pain of specific body parts in such graphic detail that my mind would wander. I would *never* be so self-involved. But I continued to nod and smile with pretended sympathy as I thought about a million other things. Arthritis was the last thing on my mind. I didn't have time for arthritis; I had better things to do. I would wait for her to pause, to catch her breath, and seize the opportunity to excuse myself.

I always knew arthritis was out there, somewhere,

lurking about, looking for a home, but I certainly did not choose arthritis for a roommate. It simply bypassed others and showed up on my doorstep, determined to move in. I was equally determined that it would go away. A strong-willed person by nature, downright stubborn according to some, I was convinced that I could prevent its destination by refusing entry. Ignore it and it will go away—move on to bother someone else. So, when I recognized the symptoms beginning to knock on my door, I wasn't so much surprised as I was unwilling to accept that it was happening.

At first, I was merely annoyed by the pain and its interfering with my life-style, and I was very successful at ignoring it. I continued my routine, constantly aware of the nagging pain but determined to go on with my life as if nothing were happening. No one really knew what I was going through, and I was proud that I was handling the situation without complaint.

Eventually the pain increased and became increasingly difficult to ignore. My family became aware of my difficulties when I found that a mundane thing, such as buttoning a coat, could be a monumental task. But when they offered to help, I was offended.

"I'll do it myself—I'm not helpless!" I'd snap.

My stubborn nature was intact, and I was still pleased with myself and my ability to go on despite the insidious pain. Determined, I fought for concentration, and through sheer willpower I blocked the pain and was able to complete simple chores that no longer seemed so simple.

A Story: The Last Thing on My Mind

My efforts fatigued me, and I grew weary of being the trooper and gutting it out. Searching for concentration, I discovered that I could no longer concentrate on anything except the pain. My strong will was taking a terrible beating, and my stubborn nature was slowly dissolving from repeated doses of humility. I reluctantly asked my family for help, then watched with resentment as they accomplished the tasks with ease.

In the next few months arthritis produced a significant change in my personality. I was not nearly so sure of my abilities. I tired easily and never seemed able to accomplish physically what my mind set out to do. I was frustrated by my laziness and laid claim to the family's most comfortable chair. The chair, once up for grabs, was now clearly mine. I became the family's resident meteorologist, able to predict the day's weather according to my difficulty in getting out of bed.

"Better take your umbrella today," I'd warn as I struggled painfully to an upright position.

Pride lost priority, and I didn't resent asking for help. My family had simply divided up my responsibilities, and I didn't even bother to ask.

I wasn't hungry, so I didn't cook. My family wouldn't starve. They could take care of themselves. How hard could it be to throw some clothes in a washer and push a button? Not nearly so noble, I began complaining more and more about the pain. I didn't bother much with my personal appearance. It was hopeless to try and look good when I felt so bad.

I didn't choose to have arthritis; it wasn't my fault. My family would just have to understand that I was a victim of a devastating disease. They didn't have to deal with it. Arthritis had chosen *me*.

Its physical presence was painfully apparent, a fierce and constant reminder that it had moved into my body. What was more subtle and, eventually, infinitely more devastating was that arthritis had also set up residence in my mind. The effect it was having on my state of mind went unchecked because it was camouflaged by the immediate and urgent physical pain. The obsession quietly grew and festered while I was preoccupied with the physical reality of pain.

I was certainly more interested in arthritis. The last thing on my mind now appeared to be the only thing on my mind. I didn't want to talk about anything else. How could I? I rarely thought about anything else.

I read all the articles about "breakthroughs" in arthritis, hoping to find a cure. I turned to family members for advice. Relatives came through with scores of home remedies and I embarked on a series of trial-and-error experiments. I wanted a quick and easy solution at any cost, both monetary and self-esteem. I overcame the embarrassment of buying alfalfa tablets and gallons of seawater. I overcame the nausea these substances produced in my system. I tried every new diet, searching for a cure, gorging myself with foods I detested while eliminating some of my favorites. I tried charging up on large doses of vitamins that charged me with little more than an urge to vomit.

A Story: The Last Thing on My Mind

Every arthritis television commercial was written specifically for me, and all over-the-counter products found their way into my medicine chest. I even bought a copper bracelet that, though it didn't help, left me no worse for the wear except for a nearly permanent green ring on my wrist.

The obsession was growing all the while and, though I spent all of my time and energy on myself and my arthritis, nothing seemed to work. The failures were piling up, and I was a disagreeable and despondent person.

I awoke one morning to realize the full extent of arthritis. The instant I opened my eyes, I felt a heavy, sinking feeling press down on me. The pain was more intense than any I had felt up to that time. I was afraid to move—afraid that I could not move. The side effects of arthritis on my mind had also reached a peak. I was filled with rage at the injustice I had been dealt. I felt as if the rage would explode and leave me a pile of bones and ashes. I wanted to lash out but there was no one to blame, so the fury turned inward and became self-hate.

The obsession had festered into a depression that seemed almost tangible. It was as if a wave of fog rolled into the room and swallowed me up. I didn't even resist it; I welcomed it. I was ready to forfeit the strong will that had once been a source of pride. Pride was something I could no longer afford and I was eager to give up, to be relieved of the responsibility of fighting arthritis. In slower and slower motion, I became slowly paralyzed, petrified as a stone. The longer I lay, the harder it was to move; the harder it was to move, the longer I lay. Totally inanimate, I began to stare into the fog, a stare focusing on nothing. I didn't care about anything or anyone. Arthritis was in control. I didn't bother to get out of bed that day.

It's not clear to me how long I was in that state of mind, a life totally centered on myself, but my family ran out of patience. They had tried to help me to deal with arthritis, but now *I* wasn't dealing with it at all. I had given up on myself, and they had given up on me. Thick walls of resentment had been built and they were simply going on about their business as if I were some sort of object in the house. Indeed, I had become such a fixture in the chair that I was little more than a piece of furniture.

At first, I was hurt by their insensitivity, but I finally realized that I wasn't a member of the family anymore. I didn't deserve to be. It had been weeks (months?) since I had asked them how they felt, or for that matter even cared. I couldn't recognize myself anymore. I was frightened by the fact that this strange person would live for the rest of my life in my body. I didn't know this person, wasn't comfortable with this person; I really *hated* this person. Yet I was the only one who would or even *could* do anything about it.

I called the relative I'd always avoided, got the name of a doctor, and made an appointment. I was very apprehensive about the visit and didn't volunteer any information. He ran me through a series of tests that

A Story: The Last Thing on My Mind

I didn't understand. I was a little frightened, but more afraid to question him about it. He began talking about medications I hadn't heard of and used terms I didn't understand. He seemed to be speaking in a foreign language. My emotions seemed to be running helter-skelter, from being angry to frustrated to embarrassed to extremely nervous. He asked me some questions that I didn't even understand, and to my surprise I burst into tears. The doctor was very kind, and I was startled by his perception.

"You've been trying to handle arthritis all by yourself, haven't you?"

"Well, yes, I guess so. I'm afraid I haven't been doing a very good job," I confessed.

"Oh, I'd say you're on your way. You're here, aren't you?" he smiled. "You obviously have the desire to help yourself, and that is the first step toward controlling arthritis. It's a little like fighting a weight problem. Weight takes time to gain—time to lose. With arthritis, *control* takes time to lose—time to gain. If you are as persistent and determined in treatment as arthritis is in taking over, you will be just fine."

The doctor handed me a stack of pamphlets containing information about arthritis. He described, in detail, a total program to be followed for six weeks that included drugs, exercises, rest, and diet. I listened very carefully and even asked some questions. When I left, I felt a little of the old me slip back with the confidence that I could do something about my situation.

I read the pamphlets as soon as I got home and was

amazed at how little I knew about a disease I had "known" about all my life. I looked up some of the terms that the doctor had used, and a lot of my fears were alleviated just by knowing that my experiences were normal.

The days that followed were tedious and monotonous, but I was very determined to follow my prescription to the letter. I exercised even when I didn't want to. I rested when I knew I should. I took my medication properly. I prepared and ate well-balanced meals. It wasn't easy to maintain such a rut, and by no means was it the most exciting six weeks of my life. But I was in control, and they were the most pleasant days I had spent for a long time.

My family definitely noticed a difference. I was renewing acquaintances and was interested in *them*. They recognized the old me coming back, fighting and spunky as ever. I even chastised them for "helping" when I didn't ask. They read some of the pamphlets, and resentments began transforming into understandings. With my newly found power, I wasn't invincible; there were bad days. But the old me was back, and I could deal with it one day at a time, knowing that my family and my doctor were on my side.

I went back to the doctor and informed him that I did not cheat, even once.

"I can tell," smiled the doctor. "You should continue the program for as long as it works. Be sure to let me know of any changes. There are lots of things we can do to help you cope with arthritis. The most important thing, though, is your attitude and determination. I don't think I have to worry," he chuckled. "You seem to be a person with a very strong will."

"You could say 'downright stubborn,'" I winked.

I went to a family reunion the other day. I caught a cousin and began to talk her ear off about my arthritis intrusion. She smiled and nodded with pretended sympathy. As I began listening to myself, I recalled an earlier conversation. I stopped talking mid-sentence, and she asked me why.

"Oh, I see someone I really need to talk to," I explained, and noticed the relief in her expression.

I walked over to the family member that I had talked—no, half listened to—a year earlier.

"How's your arthritis?" I asked.

She paused a moment and then smiled.

"You tell me."

We talked for most of the reunion, swapping stories and sharing ideas about living with arthritis. Some of the stories even seemed humorous in retrospect. She invited me to the next meeting of her support group, and I felt as though I had just met a new friend in this relative I had known for years.

We even talked about things *other* than arthritis, a subject that in past conversations we never got beyond. I discovered that we shared many interests, and we made plans to work on a project together.

I went home feeling content, in control, and planning for the future. Arthritis went home with me, but my ego was far too inflated to be bothered by it. I had better things to do. Arthritis was the last thing on my mind.

2 The Story and You

એએએએ

Well, that was an interesting little story, but what's the purpose? Possibly you identified with the narrator, and surely you recognized some of the characteristics of arthritis.

Events vary, but there is a basic plot to arthritis. You are the protagonist and arthritis is the antagonist. The agony begins when arthritis moves in with you. You already know about arthritis; it's probably in your family. You may even fear it somewhat but don't really like to think about it, and for heaven's sake you don't want to talk about it all the time. You may listen to someone else's complaints out of politeness. Then one day, you begin noticing some symptoms: annoying pains, fatigue, irritability, perhaps a loss of appetite—arthritis is knocking at your door. You have an inkling that it may be arthritis, but you ignore it. It will go

11

away. You compensate quite well for a time, but eventually the symptoms begin to wear on you. You make a self-diagnosis, and decide that it probably is arthritis. The aches and pains make you very conscious of its arrival, but the effect it has on your mind is more subtle. Arthritis can be a devastating disease, and its constant presence may overwhelm you, threatening to take over your mind as well as your body.

Instinctively, you become more curious about arthritis and will probably want to learn more about it. This natural curiosity is good unless you rely on secondhand information and home remedies. You want to cure yourself, and in your desire you may fall victim to quackery.

There is no cure for arthritis and searching for one in unproven remedies will only result in failure. Feeling like a failure can make you very depressed. Depression can be a side effect of arthritis. At this point, some decisions are necessary. In the story, the narrator had reached the bottom, and the only way to go was up. It was at this point that the narrator accepted the responsibility for arthritis. The realization that no one else could deal with arthritis was the first step in turning it into a success story, a story with a happy ending.

The narrator was lucky enough to find a doctor who saw his patient as a whole person. He knew that by taking care of the whole person, as well as the symptoms, the narrator could gain control over arthritis.

The analogy is beginning to make sense, but you're still not sure. You were probably already aware of traditional methods of treatment: drugs, exercise, and rest, but why a story?

The story introduces some new ingredients into the treatment of arthritis: patient attitude and patient responsibility.

The presence of arthritis in your body is very apparent, but what does it do to your mind? That you will probably live with arthritis for the rest of your life has to be something you think about. But how much do you think about it? Is arthritis the only thing on your mind?

Attitude can play a very important role in the treatment of arthritis. The mind and body are connected, and your state of mind can affect how you feel physically. If you see yourself as an arthritic, period, then arthritis weighs very heavily on your mind. If you realize that "arthritic" is simply one of many, many adjectives that describes you, you are on your way to shrinking arthritis to an appropriate size. What is an appropriate size? Well, it is only part of you, and so it should be considerably smaller. Some days it will shrink, some days it will grow, but it should always look up to you. You are the authority; it's your mind, your body.

No pill has yet been invented that produces a positive attitude, but if you want to help yourself and your arthritis, developing one is your responsibility.

Ah, responsibility—there's more.

You are responsible for yourself, and since arthritis is part of you, you are also responsible for it. You cannot bring it to a doctor and leave it there to be fixed. It will go home with you. You should listen to the doctor's advice and follow the treatment prescribed because he or she knows how to help you medically. But your doctor doesn't live with arthritis. You do.

It is easy to let the doctor take responsibility because it removes the burden of blame from you. The doctor is at fault, or your mother had arthritis so it's her fault. You must realize that only you are responsible, and it's not your fault either. It just is, and no one can deal with it except you. Childbirth comes to mind as an example. (Sorry, men, please try to improvise.) There is a point in childbirth at which you would like to quit, let someone else take over. But the reality is there— you cannot quit. Of all the people in the whole world, only you can give birth to that particular child at that particular moment. You are responsible. You have no choice. There are people available to help you, to hold your hand, to encourage, care, and administer medical treatment when necessary. But ultimately, you are on your own. It is painful, but what an accomplishment!

Arthritis is not very different except that the pain occurs on a daily basis. Having a baby once in a while is exciting, and the pain is gone between experiences. To deal with chronic pain is monotonous and discouraging, but if you can see your ability to conquer pain as an accomplishment, one that deserves reward, the experience may be more tolerable. You have to deal with pain. You are responsible. You have no choice. There are people available to help you, to hold your hand, to encourage, care, and administer medical treatment when necessary. But ultimately you are on your own.

So you are responsible for your attitude and how you deal with pain, but you are responsible physically as well. Mental health and physical health are very closely related. There are certain things that maintain both. These things include diet, rest, and exercise. People tend to run hard and fast until they break down. They run to the doctor, demand to be fixed, then off they go again. Sometimes this works, but eventually the machine cannot be fixed easily and spends a lot of time in the shop. Proper maintenance and preventive measures are still the best bet to keep things running smoothly. Everyone must take care of their equipment, but if you have arthritis, this maintenance schedule must be more closely adhered to. The machine has been driven hard and fast and now needs some tender loving care.

Let's put it in perspective and go back to the baby you bore. It is not likely that you are going to fill that baby's bottle with coffee or alcohol, feed it junk food, let it lie idly for long periods, or push it beyond its limit by setting it to hard labor. More likely you will see to it that it eats properly, rests comfortably, and gets some exercise. You will keep it clean and well loved. Do you do the same for yourself? Sometimes we tend to accept responsibility for others more easily than for ourselves.

Well, arthritis is your baby. Unplanned? Unwanted? A problem child? Granted. But it is there, and it will not just go away. You are responsible for controlling arthritis. The sooner you take responsibility, the sooner you gain control. It will keep knocking until you are forced to let it in. That choice is made for you. Your choice comes in what to do after it moves in.

These things are not what you want to read. You want to read that there is a new pill that you take once that cures your arthritis, and then you are on your way back to your previous life-style. The cold, hard fact is that no such pill exists. There are no easy solutions. You have to take responsibility. Once you accept responsibility for something, your duties often become clear. Arthritis is no exception.

Okay, okay, so you're responsible already! You have to change your life-style, but how? In the most basic terms, your duties are explained in the following sections:

You may want to glance at the outlines for each chapter. They will give you a brief summary and a clue to what you're getting into.

PHASE ONE

۞۞۞۞

An Education

This section is designed primarily for reference purposes and certainly is not intended to be memorized. You will, however, take note of terms that may apply to you. You may also want to look up a term or medication in the future should a doctor use one with which you are not familiar.

3 What Is Arthritis?

ᘓᘓᘓᘓ

So you have arthritis. Now what? Your basic instincts make you much more curious about the term now that it applies to you. This natural curiosity is very important. Learning as much as you can about the disease will help you to cope with it. Read, research, learn what you can. Educate yourself and your family members. Their understanding and support will also help you. Ignorance may be bliss, but it really isn't much of an excuse. Fear aggravates a problem and education alleviates fear.

Arthritis intrudes on the privacy of over thirty-six million Americans, or one in seven, to some degree or another. A more shocking statistic: arthritis moves in on someone in this country every 32 seconds! It does not discriminate, choosing all ages and both sexes, but it does seem to prefer women.

The term *arthritis* refers to over one hundred conditions of arthritis that affect the joints, bones, muscles, and connective tissue. In England, the term *rheumatism* is preferred, but arthritis has been accepted in America as a better term to cover these conditions.

The term *arthritis* means inflammation of the joint. Extremely unpredictable, arthritis can flare up for no apparent reason. Normally inflammation is an important factor in the healing reaction to an injury of body tissue. Inflammation presents itself as heat, swelling, pain, and redness in the affected area. But with arthritis, the inflammatory process becomes abnormal and out of control, actually causing damage. This overactive healing process may then make the joints difficult to move the cause distortion.

The two most common types of arthritis are osteoarthritis and rheumatoid arthritis. Nearly everyone who lives long enough will experience visits from osteoarthritis to some degree. Rheumatoid arthritis is the most common chronic type of inflammatory arthritis and may cause crippling. These two types of arthritis are generally characterized by a gradual onset. A mere annoyance at first, its insidious persistence eventually makes it difficult for a person to ignore. Although most types of arthritis have a gradual onset, some appear quite abruptly, moving in forcefully and immediately. Gout, infectious arthritis, and sometimes even rheumatoid arthritis can come on within a day or even hours.

What Is Arthritis?

Not all joint pains are arthritis. Many self-limited conditions, especially viral infections such as the flu or mononucleosis, may cause transient joint pain. This is why some chronic types of arthritis are not diagnosed until the symptoms are present for six weeks or longer.

The most common symptoms of arthritis are pain and stiffness. It can be a frustrating disease since it continues to keep a person guessing. The person may awaken stiff and in pain and gradually become more limber with movement, only to be assaulted by a repeat attack of pain and stiffness toward the day's end. The duration of morning stiffness, as in arthritis characterized by active inflammation of thirty minutes or more, can be used as a guide for the disease's activity and help in diagnosis. Changes in weather, emotional upset, and other stress may also be responsible for day to day fluctuation. Because these conditions fluctuate daily, activity must be observed for long periods of time to chart trends of the disease.

Just as daily fluctuations influence the characteristics of the disease, arthritis may fluctuate in totality. A spontaneous remission can occur with the person experiencing a complete absence of symptoms. This remission can occur by itself, and not because of or in spite of any method of treatment. Remission may last days, weeks, months, years, and in rare cases a lucky person may see arthritis move out for good. Remission, however, is rarely permanent, and symptoms usually return. A relapse presents itself in the form of recurring symptoms, often more severe than previously experienced.

Besides osteoarthritis and rheumatoid arthritis, there are over a hundred other types of arthritis, and an accurate diagnosis of the specific type is essential for proper treatment. Often, the family physician, after careful testing and a thorough examination, can make the diagnosis of many types of arthritis. X rays and lab tests may aid in the diagnosis, and sometimes a doctor specializing in arthritis may be needed to help diagnose and prescribe treatment.

Treatment involves a combination of drugs, therapy, exercise, rest, diet, and possible surgery. Treatment is as individual and personal as the person who has arthritis. It is important to establish a good relationship with a doctor who then prescribes an appropriate program that suits the individual needs of each arthritis patient.

The cause of most types of arthritis is unknown, but infections and heredity are possible factors. To date, no specific microorganism has been found to explain all types of arthritis. Infectious arthritis can be caused by a specific bacteria, virus, or fungus, but this represents a very small percentage of the cases of arthritis.

Heredity does play an important part in some cases, including gout, osteoarthritis, rheumatoid arthritis, systemic lupus erythematosus, and ankylosing spondylitis. This does not mean that people with these types of arthritis in their family history will always develop the disorder. But the presence of a genetic marker does mean that the person is predisposed to the condition.

Arthritis is the nation's number one crippling disease, but there are now very effective methods of treatment that improve the overall health of persons with arthritis. Following a program of doctor-prescribed treatment will not cure the disease, but it will make living with arthritis a more tolerable existence and enable a person to continue a happy and productive life-style.

4 Doctor Talk: Tests and Terms

Antinuclear Antibody (ANA)

Blood Count (Hemoglobin and Hematocrit)

Complement (C-3, C-4, CH-50)

Creatinine

DNA Antibody

Genetic Marker (Tissue Typing)

Immune Complexes

Immune System

Osteoporosis

Platelet Count

Rheumatoid Factor

Salicylate Level

Erythrocyte Sedimentation Rate (ESR, Sed Rate)

Synovitis

Uric Acid

Urinalysis

White Blood Count (WBC)

❧❧❧❧

Perhaps you will be lucky enough to find a doctor who sees you as a whole person, but even if you don't there's no reason to despair. You see yourself as a whole person, so make the doctor see you that way. In the story, the narrator was afraid to ask questions. That simply reinforces a doctor's inclination to treat symptoms only; that is the doctor's job. But if you ask questions, are interested in what the doctor is doing, project some personality, the doctor will naturally begin seeing you as a whole person.

So one of the most important things that you can do for yourself and your arthritis is to establish open communication with your doctor. Unfortunately doctors are bilingual, and their medical foreign language can confuse the communication system. Therefore, it is important that you understand the terminology the doctor is likely to use in discussing your arthritis with you. Various labels used to identify tests, medications, conditions, and even types of arthritis can be confusing and intimidating. But, like foreign words, they will blend naturally into your vocabulary if you learn their definitions and use them in conversation. Remember, it took the doctor years of study to learn this language, and you need to learn only those terms pertinent to your condition.

Successful treatment of arthritis can depend on your knowledge of the disease and your ability to help yourself. Never consider questioning the doctor as a nuisance. You should be as knowledgeable as possible about what you have, what you are doing about it, and why. Getting answers to these questions greatly improves your ability to deal with arthritis. This communication with your physician is imperative, but it can be achieved only if you know what your doctor is talking about.

You may need to undergo several tests that will enable the doctor to diagnose and monitor your disease. By familiarizing yourself with these terms and tests, you can better understand what the doctor is doing and why.

Antinuclear Antibody (ANA)

The ANA is a laboratory test that detects a variety of antibodies that the body makes against substances, including proteins, inside the cells of the body. The ANA is reported as positive or negative. Positive tests are reported as *titers* (tye′tur) (1:20, 1:40, 1:80, etc.), with higher titers being more positive. The ANA is most useful as a screening test for a form of arthritis

27

called systemic lupus erythematosus (SLE) that we will be discussing. It is positive in ninety plus percent of people who have SLE, though a positive ANA test is not a specific finding for SLE or any other form of arthritis.

Blood Count (Hemoglobin and Hematocrit)

The blood count is a common blood test that measures the total number of red blood cells and the levels of hemoglobin and hematocrit. A reduction of red blood cells or the level of hemoglobin and hematocrit is called *anemia*. Anemia is common with many types of arthritis. Anemia may also be due to blood loss caused by certain types of medications, such as aspirin or other nonsteroidal anti-inflammatory drugs. The physician will monitor the blood count during the course of arthritis. While on drugs like gold, D-penicillamine, azathioprine, or methotrexate, the blood count, as well as the white blood and platelet count, may need to be measured at regular intervals.

Complement (C-3, C-4, CH-50)

The doctor may order a complement test. Complement is the number of normal blood proteins produced by the liver. Some components of complement are important in fighting some forms of infection. Complement plays a role in the overactive inflammatory process of arthritis. In some forms of arthritis, especially SLE, complement levels may fall below normal and indicate the activity of the disease. Rarely, a person is born without a certain component of complement, which may predispose the person to infection or to development of autoimmune diseases like SLE.

Creatinine

Creatinine (kree-at'i-neen) is a blood component that indicates the kidney's ability to filter waste products from the bloodstream. Because the kidneys may be involved with some forms of arthritis, especially SLE, vasculitis, and scleroderma, the creatinine may need to be measured to check for kidney damage. Rarely, nonsteroidal anti-inflammatory drugs may damage the kidneys, causing the creatinine to rise. Therefore, creatinine tests may be necessary after diagnosis to monitor potential kidney damage. The higher the creatinine, the more kidney damage is indicated. Normal creatinine level is less than 1.5 mg.

DNA Antibody

DNA antibody forms against DNA in the body's cells. The doctor uses the DNA antibody test to help diagnose certain types of arthritis. The presence of DNA antibody in high levels is a strong indication of SLE. It was once thought that SLE was the only form of arthritis that had DNA antibodies. It is now known that other forms of arthritis, such as rheumatoid arthritis, and other medical conditions, have DNA antibodies in low levels. The doctor may use this test in diagnosing your disease.

Genetic Marker (Tissue Typing)

Great strides have been made by the identification of the HLA system. This refers to the presence of certain markers that can be detected on chromosomes by lab testing. Each person gets two sets of these markers from their parents. The presence of certain markers may predispose the individual to develop certain forms of arthritis. The strongest association has been the presence of HLA-B-27 in certain forms of arthritis, especially ankylosing spondylitis and Reiter's syndrome. As high as 8% of the general population has a positive HLA-B-27. But people with this genetic marker don't necessarily develop these forms of arthritis.

Immune Complexes

Immune complexes are like large blocks with many small attachments. The small attachments are antibodies against that particular block. Everybody forms these complexes daily, but they are normally filtered from the body by the liver and spleen. DNA-anti-DNA is one of the best known immune complexes, occurring most commonly in SLE. If not filtered by the liver or spleen, immune complexes can get deposited in body tissue and injure the kidneys (nephritis), joints (arthritis), or blood vessels (vasculitis).

Immune System

In simple terms, the immune system is the body's defense system against foreign invaders like bacteria and viruses. The defense system is made up of a variety of cells, including lymphocytes. In many cases of arthritis, the lymphocytes, for reasons unknown, become confused and rather than defend the body actually attack it. The immune system attacking itself is the basis of autoimmune diseases like SLE and rheumatoid arthritis. This sets off a variety of reactions that leads to inflammation and eventually damages joints and tissues.

Osteoporosis

Osteoporosis (os"tee-o-po-ro'sis) is a common medical disorder often mistaken as a form of arthritis. Though not a form of arthritis, osteoporosis is associated with many types of arthritis. Osteoporosis is a condition caused by a gradual loss of calcium that produces softening of the bones, especially those of the spine and hips. Osteoporosis most commonly affects women after menopause. Fractures occur more easily since the bones are soft. Treatment of osteoporosis includes calcium replacement, 1000–1500 mg/day (plus vitamin D), and regular exercise. Using estrogens and other medications are sometimes recommended to prevent the condition.

Platelet Count

Platelets are small cells in the blood that help the blood to clot. When the platelet count gets too low, there is a risk of uncontrolled bleeding. Low platelet count can be caused by some forms of arthritis, particularly SLE, and by some medications, especially disease-modifying (gold, penicillamine) and cytotoxic (azathioprine, cyclophosphamide, methotrexate) agents. The platelet count is monitored frequently while one is on these medications.

Rheumatoid Factor

Rheumatoid factor is an antibody, detected by a blood test, that is most often used to help diagnose rheumatoid arthritis. This antibody is present in 60–80%

of adults with rheumatoid arthritis. Up to 20% of people over 65, without arthritis, have a positive test for rheumatoid factor in low levels. Therefore, the presence of a positive rheumatoid factor is nonspecific and doesn't necessarily mean one has rheumatoid arthritis.

Salicylate Level

Salicylate (sa-lis'i-late) level is a blood test the doctor uses to determine how much aspirin is in the system. Because everyone is different, this test may help determine the correct dosage of aspirin for each person. A therapeutic blood level is 15–30 mg/100 ml to achieve full anti-inflammatory effects from the aspirin. This test will also reveal aspirin intoxication (someone taking too much aspirin).

Erythrocyte Sedimentation Rate (ESR, Sed Rate)

The erythrocyte (e-rith'ro-sight) sedimentation rate is a common blood test that many doctors do in their office. The level of the sed rate can indicate how active certain types of arthritis are, such as rheumatoid arthritis, SLE, and temporal arteritis. Usually, the more inflammation the higher the sed rate. Normal sed rate is 0–15 mm/hr for men, 0–20 mm/hr for women.

Finding out the sed rate can help determine the activity of inflammation in the body.

Synovitis

Synovitis (sin"o-vye′tis) means inflammation of the synovium, the membrane that lines the joints. The physician uses this term when he or she detects swelling, warmth, or redness while examining the joints.

Uric Acid

Uric (yoor′ick) acid is a normal substance produced in the body as cells break down and die. There is a blood test that measures the level of uric acid. Normal levels vary depending on the lab where the test is done. Elevation of the uric acid in the bloodstream is seen in the majority of people suffering from gouty arthritis and usually needs to be treated with drugs. Elevation of the uric acid level also occurs in many people not suffering from gout. Excessive alcohol, diuretics (water pills), and small doses of aspirin (2–4/day) can elevate the level of uric acid.

Urinalysis

Urinalysis refers to a variety of tests performed on urine. In arthritis, urinalysis is important to detect the presence of red cells, protein, and abnormal cells in the urine. When a patient is on certain medications, especially the disease-modifying agents (gold, penicillamine), regular urine checks for protein and blood are necessary to detect early side effects affecting the kidneys. Regular urinalysis is also useful to detect kidney involvement in conditions such as SLE or progressive systemic sclerosis (scleroderma).

White Blood Count (WBC)

The white blood cells are produced in the bone marrow and are important in fighting infections. A decrease in the white blood count predisposes a person to infections. There are several types of white blood cells, which can be distinguished when seen through a microscope. These different forms of white cells behave differently according to the kind of infection present. The white blood count of a patient with arthritis may decrease because of the toxicity of certain medications, especially disease-modifying agents (gold, penicillamine) and cytotoxic agents (azathioprine, methotrexate, cyclophosphamide). Regular monitoring of the white blood count is necessary if one is on disease-modifying and cytotoxic agents.

Well, you've learned some fancy words, and it wasn't too bad. As usual, the fancy words have relatively simple meanings. Now that you know some medical lingo, you can ask more questions about your disease. Ask your doctor, "How's my sed rate, doc?" Only by knowing what is normal can you know if yours is abnormal, and by how much.

5 Your Medicine Chest

Unproven Remedies

Drugs
Aspirin
Analgesics
Nonsteroidal Anti-Inflammatory Drugs (NSAIDS)
Corticosteroids (Steroids, Cortisone)
Disease-Modifying Drugs
Hydroxychloroquine (Plaquenil)
Gold (Solganal, Myochrysine)
D-Penicillamine (Cuprimine, Depen)
Cytotoxic Drugs
Azathioprine (Imuran)
Cyclophosphamide (Cytoxan)
Methotrexate
Tricyclic Medications
Medications for Gout
Colchicine
Allopurinol
Probenecid

Investigational Therapy
Lymph Node Irradiation
Plasmapheresis

Surgery

చచచచ

Unproven Remedies

Arthritis sufferers truly suffer, which makes them most vulnerable to claims promising to end the pain permanently. No one blames an arthritis sufferer for wishing this. Indeed, many try to fulfill this wish. Quackery abounds and, well intentioned or not, the ducks keep quacking. Unproven remedies cost a lot of money, about a billion dollars a year. It is estimated that for every dollar spent on legitimate arthritis research, twenty-five dollars will be spent on unproven remedies. Though many home remedies are not harmful, some could prove dangerous. To avoid being victimized, a person with arthritis must be informed of the facts.

First, there is no cure for arthritis, and when there is it will not be any secret formula. It will be a great day, and the whole country will be quite aware of it. Anything that claims to be a *cure* for arthritis should make you extremely skeptical.

A well-balanced diet is a good idea for everyone, but there is no scientific proof that any specific type of diet plays a role in curing arthritis. Abundant sales of special health foods make the promoter feel very good, but the food will offer little relief to the arthritis sufferer taking it. Special clinics are very special only in their money making abilities. Any program they offer to cure arthritis should be avoided. There are many devices on the market claiming exclusive breakthroughs in curing arthritis. But jewelry is jewelry, and vibrators can feel as good to an arthritis sufferer as they can to anyone else.

Unproven remedies are successful because the consumer targeted is often desperate. A frequent marketing technique for these products is the testimonial, which is effective because the people involved may truly believe in the product. Arthritis is a disease that has spontaneous remissions. That a remission occurred at the time the person began wearing the copper bracelet is purely coincidence. But it is difficult to convince the person of that until a relapse occurs. The other factor is called the *placebo effect*. This means that the person believes it will work, and by mind over matter, so to speak, it does. No one really knows the full capability of the mind, but this phenomenon occurs in other medical areas besides arthritis. The placebo effect is usually temporary, and the "cure" turns out to be another tried and untrue story.

Another category of unproven remedies is drugs, which may be the most potentially dangerous. Do not take any drug for arthritis without first consulting a physician or pharmacist to discover its contents. You may be paying an exorbitant amount of money for sugar, or the drug may contain ingredients potentially harmful to you. For example, if you already take prescribed medication for your arthritis, taking additional over-the-counter drugs may cause drug interactions. If "doctor talk" was impressive, a doctor's knowledge of drugs is even more impressive. If he or she hasn't heard of a certain new "cure-all" drug, nobody has. There are plenty of available drugs that are very effective in the treatment of arthritis. Ask your doctor which ones are right for you.

Drugs

Get ready for some strange words. It is time to discuss the many medications used to treat arthritis. Many people consume drugs, whose names they may or may not be able to pronounce, without really knowing what these drugs are, or what they do. This is one reason you must have faith in your doctor. But don't rely totally on faith. Ask about your medication, what it does, what it could possibly do, why you are taking it, and how it works. Many drugs are slow acting, and if you are aware of this, it helps you to be patient with your progress.

An arthritis medicine chest can be a full one indeed, and it is up to you and your physician to decide which medications will be stocked in your cabinet.

Aspirin

Aspirin is the most common drug used to treat arthritis, and it is effective in relieving pain and reducing inflammation. These two effects of aspirin occur at different dosages. Taking two aspirin tablets will relieve pain, such as headache. But to reduce inflammation, eight to twenty aspirin a day are necessary. This dose will vary from person to person, and to achieve accurate dosage your blood salicylate level should be measured. Steady dosage is essential to keep inflammation under control.

Taking ten or more aspirin a day can become expensive. Plain aspirin is the important compound, and advertised brands will cost more. Other brands of aspirin, such as buffered, enteric-coated, or nonacetylated aspirin may be necessary because of common gastrointestinal side effects from taking plain aspirin. About 50% of people taking plain aspirin will have gastrointestinal upset. This can be reduced by taking the aspirin with food, which is recommended for most arthritis medications. Some patients taking full doses of aspirin may experience ringing of the ears or decreased hearing. This can be a sign of toxicity, and a physician should be alerted of these side effects. Other side effects of taking aspirin include allergic reactions ranging from hives to difficulty in breathing from uncontrolled asthma.

Enteric-coated aspirin is especially good for reducing gastrointestinal upset. Ecotrin, Easpirin, and Encaprin are the more reliable enteric-coated forms of aspirin. Ecotrin is marketed as 325- or 500-mg tablets, so you must be sure you're getting the proper dosage when buying it. Easpirin is available only by prescription and each tablet is 975 mg (equivalent to three regular aspirin). Therefore the dosage is three to six tablets per day. Encaprin is a recently marketed capsule that contains 325 or 500 mg of coated granules of aspirin. These granules are slowly released, allowing the drug to be given twice a day. The normal dose is two to four capsules, twice a day.

Zorprin is a sustained release formula of a plain aspirin compound that has properties like that of an enteric-coated aspirin. Each Zorprin tablet contains 800 mg of aspirin. An advantage is that it is taken two or three times a day.

Nonacetylated salicylates were developed to reduce gastrointestinal upset and stomach bleeding associated with plain aspirin. There are many formulas, but some of the more common ones are Trilisate, Disalcid, and Magan.

Diflunisal (Dolobid) is an aspirin derivative recently on the market. It too produces less gastrointestinal upset and bleeding than plain aspirin. Dolobid had been used for pain relief only but has recently been approved for use as an anti-inflammatory agent. The usual dose is 250–500 mg a day.

Analgesics

The analgesics are designed strictly to relieve pain of arthritis. This class of drugs possesses no anti-inflammatory properties. Their advantage over aspirin is that they rarely have gastrointestinal side effects. There are many analgesics available; some are over-the-counter while others must be obtained by a prescription.

Acetaminophen (as"e-tuh-mee'no-fen) (Tylenol, Datril, Panadol, etc.) is the best known over-the-counter analgesic. It comes in either 325-mg or 500-mg strengths. Normal dose is two tablets every four to six hours as needed for pain. One should not exceed eight extra-strength (500 mg) acetaminophen tablets in a day because there is a risk of liver damage with over-dosage. Acetaminophen can be taken with aspirin or nonsteroidal anti-inflammatory drugs (NSAIDS) to help control pain from arthritis.

Ibuprofen (eye-bew'pro-fen) (Advil, Nuprin) is a drug that just received FDA approval for over-the-counter use as an analgesic. It comes in a 200-mg tablet. As is discussed in the next section, ibuprofen (Motrin, Rufen) is a very popular drug of the non-steroidal anti-inflammatory drugs (NSAIDS). At the 200-mg dosage, it is intended to be taken every four to six hours as needed for pain. At this dose, it will not relieve inflammation. The major caution about ibuprofen is that it should not be taken as an analgesic while taking one of the other NSAIDS without consulting your physician.

Propoxyphene (pro-pock'see-feen) (Darvon) is one of the most common narcotic analgesics used to help control pain. It is very useful in helping control the more severe pain associated with arthritis. Darvon is available in many forms, including Darvon-65 (propoxyphene, aspirin, and caffeine), Darvon with A.S.A. (propoxyphene and aspirin), and Darvocet-N-50 and 100 (propoxyphene and acetaminophen).

The usual dosage of Darvon compound is one tablet or capsule every four hours as needed for pain. Remember, propoxyphene is a narcotic, and therefore can be habit forming. Also, excessive intake can cause overdosage. Alcohol intake should be limited when taking propoxyphene or, for that matter, any narcotic analgesic because of the additive effects of the two. Plain Darvon or Darvocet-N-100 can be taken with aspirin or the NSAIDS.

Codeine (ko′deen) is the other common narcotic analgesic that is used to control more severe types of pain. It too is quite useful in treating severe pain associated with arthritis.

Codeine is available as plain tablets or more commonly combined with aspirin (Empirin No. 2, 3, 4) or acetaminophen (Tylenol No. 1, 2, 3, 4). The number after the compound tells how much codeine is in the drug. Number 2 has 15 mg of codeine, number 3 has 30 mg, and number 4 has 60 mg.

The usual dosage is one or two tablets every four to six hours as needed for severe pain. Long-term use of codeine can be habit forming, and it should not be used with excessive alcohol or sedative intake. Codeine can be taken safely with either aspirin or the NSAIDS.

Nonsteroidal Anti-Inflammatory Drugs (NSAIDS)

The class of nonsteroidal anti-inflammatory drugs is adding new members all the time. These drugs are not cortisone or cortisone-derivative drugs. They have properties similar to aspirin in the treatment of arthritis. They are effective anti-inflammatory and analgesic agents but are *not* superior to aspirin. Their major advantage over aspirin is reduced side effects. People unable to tolerate aspirin are usually able to tolerate one of the NSAIDS. Compared to 50% of people using plain aspirin, about 20% of patients using NSAIDS will experience gastrointestinal upset. The side effects include nausea, heartburn, gas, abdominal pain, and bloating. About 1–2% of people treated with NSAIDS may develop an ulcer. The gastrointestinal side effects can be reduced by taking these drugs with food or antacids. A patient with a history of recent ulcers should use these drugs with caution and under the direction of a physician. People with uncontrolled asthma, or who have a history of hives and asthma when taking aspirin, should not take these drugs.

Other side effects of the NSAID group include headache, dizziness, and light-headedness. These effects are more common with indomethacin (in"do-meth'uh-sin) (Indocin). Skin rash and blurred vision are rare. Fluid retention with ankle swelling can also occur, but this effect is more common with phenyl-butazone (fen"il-bew'tuh-zone) (Butazolidin) and ox-yphenbutazone (ock"si-fen-bew-tuh-zone) (Tandearil). Diarrhea may also occur and is most common with meclofenamate (meck"lo-fen'uh-mate) (Meclomen).

A unique characteristic of the NSAIDS is that their effectiveness varies from person to person. For example, ibuprofen may work wonders for one person and yet do very little to relieve another person with the same type of arthritis. The physician may need to try several drugs to find the right one for the individual patient.

Patients frequently ask "How long do I need to take the NSAID before I can expect results?" Most experts say that if a patient shows no clinical improvement after two weeks, he or she is not likely to be helped by that drug.

NSAIDS will reduce stiffness, swelling, and pain when taken regularly. However, they do differ in their duration of action. One type may be taken once a day, while others may need to be taken two, three, or even four times a day to be effective. The appropriate dosage will be outlined by the physician prescribing the particular drug.

Taking aspirin in addition to any of the NSAIDS is generally not recommended. A combination of the two should be taken only under the direction of a physician.

Cost remains a major drawback of NSAIDS, with a month's prescription averaging between $30 and $45. The expense is worthwhile if the drug works, but it may strain the budget when a patient is taking other drugs as well. Many pharmacies will give a discounted price on bottles of 100.

Listed below are the nonsteroidal anti-inflammatory drugs presently available. As many as a dozen or more new agents may be available within the next two years.

Ibuprofen (Motrin, Rufen)	400–600 mg	3–4 times a day
Naproxen (Naprosyn, Anaprox)	250–500 mg	2 times a day
Fenoprofen (Nalfon)	200–600 mg	3–4 times a day
Indomethacin (Indocin)	25–75 mg	3–4 times a day
Indomethacin (Indocin SR)	75 mg	1–2 times a day
Indomethacin suppositories (Indocin)	50 mg	1–2 times a day
Tolmetin (Tolectin)	200–400 mg	3–4 times a day
Sulindac (Clinoril)	150–200 mg	2 times a day
Phenylbutazone (Butazolidin)	100 mg	3 times a day
Oxyphenbutazone (Tandearil)	100 mg	3 times a day
Meclofenamate (Meclomen)	50–100 mg	4 times a day
Piroxicam (Feldene)	10–20 mg	Once a day

Corticosteroids (Steroids, Cortisone)

Corticosteroids (kor"ti-ko-steer'oyd) are better known as steroids or cortisone. Cortisone and hydrocortisone are hormones normally produced by the body's adrenal gland. These hormones are important in helping the body deal with stress, such as from a surgery, an injury, or an infection. In arthritis, the amount of inflammation or injury to a joint may be more than the body's natural hormones can handle, and the hormones may need to be supplemented. Corticosteroids used in the treatment of arthritis are very potent agents in relieving inflammation and blocking the immune system from producing destructive antibodies. There are many different preparations, including:

Cortisone (kor'ti-sone)

Hydrocortisone

Prednisone (pred'ni-sohn)
Prednisolone (pred-nis'uh-lohn)

Dexamethasone (deck"suh-meth'uh-sone)
Triamcinolone (trye"am-sin'o-lone)
Fluocinolone (floo"o-sin'uh-lohn)
Betamethasone (bay"tuh-meth'uh-sone)

Corticosteroids should not be used in the majority of types of arthritis. Systemic lupus erythematosus, some cases of rheumatoid arthritis, vasculitis, polymyositis, temporal arteritis, and a few others will benefit from these drugs. Corticosteroids are available in many forms: pill, cream, injection into a joint, injection into a vein or muscle, and solution to be used in the eye.

Corticosteroids cause numerous side effects, most of which occur with long-term use, meaning months to years. Some common side effects are increased appetite and weight gain, rounded face, easy bruising, lowered resistance to infection, and stomach upset. Weakening of muscles and precipitation or aggravation of diabetes are other possible side effects. Softening of the bones (osteoporosis) may occur and may lead to compression of the spine. Emotional liability, acne, increased body hair, cataracts, and salt and water retention, leading to swelling of the ankles or aggravated hypertension, are other potential side effects with corticosteroids. The side effects of corticosteroids are most frequent with long-term daily doses exceeding the equivalent of 10 mg of prednisone.

Except for possibly osteoporosis and a few others, many of the above side effects can be reduced by taking the corticosteroids on alternate days. But alternate day use is not always possible, and when used every day corticosteroids should be taken with food whenever possible, as a single dose in the morning.

It is essential that these drugs are not abruptly discontinued after long-term use. The body's capability to make cortisone hormones is suppressed after long-term use, and the drugs should be withdrawn gradually. The body's inability to produce these hormones may pose a danger in stressful periods, such as surgery, infection, or trauma. Wearing a medical alert identification piece is recommended for patients on corticosteroids.

Disease-Modifying Drugs

Hydroxychloroquine (Plaquenil)

Hydroxychloroquine (high-drock"see-klo'ro-queen) is a disease-modifying drug from the antimalarial class.

It is useful in treating rheumatoid arthritis and systemic lupus erythematosus.

Hydroxychloroquine is a slow-acting drug, requiring 8–12 weeks before most patients notice improvement. Like other disease-modifying agents, it is capable of bringing the disease under control.

In general, hydroxychloroquine is less potent and has fewer side effects than gold or penicillamine in the treatment of rheumatoid arthritis and should be tried first. In milder cases of SLE, hydroxychloroquine can be tried before corticosteroids.

Side effects include skin rash, nausea, vomiting, diarrhea, muscle weakness, and headaches. Eye toxicity is the most feared side effect of hydroxychloroquine. The drug may cause deposits in the cornea, producing blurred vision and difficulty in focusing. These side effects go away when the drug is stopped. Hydroxychloroquine may also cause deposits in the retina, which if undetected can cause irreversible damage. Avoiding injury to the retina requires regular eye examinations by an ophthalmologist. Baseline examination, reexamination every four to six months, and the proper dosage make this side effect very rare. The usual dosage of hydroxychloroquine is 200–400 mg a day, depending on the patient's weight.

Gold (Solganal, Myochrysine)

Gold compounds are one of the oldest forms of treatment for rheumatoid arthritis. Why and how gold compounds work is still not completely understood.

Failure to respond to conservative therapy is the most common indication that gold compounds should be used. Early, destructive disease seen on X rays and a very high titer rheumatoid factor with involvement of other body organs may also be indications for gold therapy. Most physicians will wait at least six months after the onset of the arthritis before starting gold because of the possibility of spontaneous remission.

All disease-modifying drugs are slow in producing desired results. Most people will notice no difference in symptoms for the first month or two after starting gold, and a successful response has to be measured over a long period of time.

Gold cannot repair damage already done by rheumatoid arthritis, but it can bring the disease under control and may help prevent further joint damage.

Generally speaking, of every ten patients treated with gold shots, six will get a good response, and one to two of the six will get a major remission. At least two will have to stop the drug because of side effects, and the remaining two will not get any response. Unfortunately, there is no good way to predict what is likely to happen to a particular patient.

Gold is injected into the muscle. The dosage is low

in the beginning and is gradually increased up to 50 mg a week. Most people are treated weekly to a total dose of 1000 mg. In the absence of severe side effects, and if there has been improvement, the gold compounds are continued and the interval between shots gradually widened, such as every two weeks for three months, then every three weeks, and so on. A pill form of gold compound called auranofin, which will be available soon, appears to have fewer severe side effects than injectable gold.

Side effects with gold treatment include skin rash, kidney damage, and damage to the bone marrow.

Skin rash is the most common side effect. It occurs anywhere on the body, including the mouth. The skin rash characteristically produces an itching sensation. A patient's complaining of a metallic taste in the mouth may indicate a reaction.

Evidence of kidney damage includes the presence of red blood cells and albumin in the urine. This condition can be kept in check by regular urine tests. Kidney damage is almost always reversible.

Finally, gold can damage bone marrow, preventing it from making white blood cells and platelets. White blood cells help to fight infections, and platelets clump together to form clots to stop bleeding. Damage can be evaluated by doing regular white blood cell and platelet counts before further gold treatment is administered.

Since gold and other disease-modifying drugs are slow in acting, they are to be given with aspirin,

NSAIDS, or corticosteroids to alleviate pain and inflammation in the meantime.

D-Penicillamine (Cuprimine, Depen)

D-penicillamine (dee-pen"i-sil'uh-meen) is a distant relative of penicillin. In effect it in no way resembles penicillin, and people who are allergic to penicillin are able to take D-penicillamine.

D-penicillamine is a slow-acting agent capable of bringing rheumatoid arthritis under control. Most people will not notice improvement for three to six months.

Generally, two-thirds of patients treated with D-penicillamine show improvement. People who have failed to respond to gold compounds or who have a relapse while on gold have just as good a chance of responding to D-penicillamine as those who did not receive gold.

Once again, side effects may limit the use of D-penicillamine. Skin rash and loss of taste are common side effects. Upset stomach, nausea, and poor appetite may also occur. Sores in the mouth may occur but will usually go away if the dose is lowered. Kidney damage with protein and blood in urine, and bone marrow suppression, with lowering of white count and platelet count, remain serious potential side effects. Rarely, D-penicillamine can induce immunologic diseases, such as systemic lupus erythematosus, myasthenia gravis, polymyositis, and Goodpasture's syndrome. Regular monitoring of the urinalysis and the white blood and platelet counts is essential while taking D-penicillamine.

The normal starting dose of D-penicillamine is 125–250 mg a day. An increased dose can be made after several months, but the total daily dosage should not exceed 1000 mg.

Cytotoxic Drugs

Azathioprine (Imuran)

Azathioprine (az"uh-thigh'o-preen) is one of a group of drugs called cytotoxic drugs that have been found useful in treating some forms of arthritis. It is approved by the FDA for treatment of rheumatoid arthritis that is not responding to other forms of therapy. Azathioprine is sometimes used in treating systemic lupus erythematosus, polymyositis, vasculitis, and other serious forms of arthritis.

Azathioprine is a powerful inhibitor of the body's immune system. It blocks the production of antibodies that cause some forms of arthritis, such as rheumatoid arthritis, SLE, and polymyositis.

Azathioprine is usually used in addition to other drugs. Special caution must be exercised when it is used with allopurinol, a drug commonly used to treat gout, because allopurinol interferes with the body's clearance ability, which may cause toxic accumulation of azathioprine.

Azathioprine comes in pill form with a 25- or 50-mg strength. The starting dose depends on the patient's weight and the condition that is being treated.

The most common side effects are nausea, vomiting, and heartburn. Hair loss and skin rash can occur, and there is an increased frequency of infections. Damage to bone marrow and liver are potential side effects that must be carefully monitored. There is a small but very real risk of developing cancer after long-term use of azathioprine. White blood and platelet counts should be monitored regularly while taking azathioprine.

Cyclophosphamide (Cytoxan)

Cyclophosphamide (sigh"klo-fos'fuh-mide) is another potent member of the cytotoxic drugs. It is not approved by the FDA for any type of arthritis, but it is used in some of the more serious forms of immune diseases, including vasculitis, Wegener's granulomatosis, SLE, polymyositis, and other related conditions. In some of these conditions, cyclophosphamide has saved lives.

Cyclophosphamide works like azathioprine by inhibiting the immune system from making antibodies. It is also capable of blocking inflammation that may destroy joints and tissue.

Cyclophosphamide is most commonly given in pill form once a day. It can also be injected into the vein in more severe conditions. The dose varies according to the patient's body weight and the condition being treated.

Cyclophosphamide is often given with corticosteroids, which allows the dose of both drugs to be kept lower than if each were given alone.

Side effects from cyclophosphamide are common and may require discontinuing the drug. Nausea, vomiting, and loss of appetite are the most common side effects. Damage to the bone marrow can occur, becoming apparent with easy bruising or a low white blood count. Irritation and inflammation of the bladder may cause pain and blood with urination. It is essential to drink plenty of fluids while taking cyclophosphamide to help prevent this side effect. Finally, loss of hair, scarring of the lung, and sterility of ovaries and testes may occur. There is no guarantee that fertility will return when the drug is stopped.

Methotrexate

Methotrexate (meth"o-treck'sate) is another of the cytotoxic drugs. Although it has been used for many years by some physicians for certain types of arthritis, it is not approved by the FDA.

Methotrexate may be used in cases of rheumatoid arthritis, polymyositis, severe psoriatic arthritis, severe Reiter's syndrome, and other related conditions that do not respond to more conservative methods of treatment. Methotrexate inhibits the immune system from making antibodies that can damage joints and tissue, and it will also reduce inflammation that contributes to the damage.

Methotrexate is most often used in pill form but may be given by injection into a muscle or a vein. For treatment of rheumatoid arthritis, the dose is 7–15 mg, given one day a week.

Methotrexate is usually used in addition to other medications, such as NSAIDS and corticosteroids.

The most common side effects are nausea, vomiting, and loss of appetite. Loss of hair, skin rash, and inflammation of the mouth may also occur. Damage to bone marrow is a potential side effect, causing low white blood count and increased risk of infection. Scarring and inflammation of the lung can occur, though uncommon. A yearly chest X ray is recommended to monitor this side effect. Sterility of ovaries and testes, possibly irreversible, is a potential side effect. Inflammation and scarring of the liver is a serious side effect. The scarring of the liver cannot always be predicted by blood tests. A liver biopsy may be required to detect early scarring in those patients who have been on the drug for several years. Abstaining from alcohol and avoiding excessive weight gain may reduce the risk of liver scarring.

Tricyclic Medications

Tricyclic medications are a class of drugs that are used at high doses (150 mg per day) in treating depression. In the last five years, much has been learned about using low doses (10–50 mg per day) to treat chronic pain syndromes, including some types of arthritis.

These drugs seem to exert a beneficial effect on the central pain center in the brain called the thalamus. In the thalamus, the tricyclic drugs seem to inhibit certain pain pathways. Disrupted sleep is often improved by the tricyclic medications because of their sedative effect. This is useful for fibromyalgia and rheumatoid arthritis.

Amitriptyline (am"i-trip'ti-leen) is the tricyclic drug most frequently used for the treatment of chronic pain syndromes. Many other preparations may be useful.

A major advantage of these drugs is that they are not habit forming and can be used indefinitely. The side effects include drowsiness, dryness of the mouth, blurring of vision, and sometimes difficulty with urination. The usual dose is 10–50 mg given at bedtime.

Medications for Gout

Colchicine

Colchicine (kol'chi-seen) is a useful drug for reducing inflammation associated with a gout attack. It interferes with the operation of certain white blood cells responsible for the inflammation.

Colchicine can be given by mouth or injected into the vein (intravenous). When given by mouth, the dosage is one tablet every hour until improvement or side effects occur. The total daily dose should not exceed 12 tablets. The intravenous method may be useful for the hospitalized patient with a gout attack who can't take pills by mouth. Colchicine is most useful in helping to prevent gout attacks. The usual dosage is 0.6 mg twice day.

Side effects, especially diarrhea, limit the treatment of acute gout attacks with colchicine. The incidence of diarrhea is much less with the twice-a-day dosage.

Allopurinol

Allopurinol (al″o-pew′ri-nol) is used to reduce the serum uric acid level, thereby reducing the risk of recurrent gout attacks. Allopurinol inhibits a certain enzyme responsible for the production of uric acid.

The usage dosage is 300–600 mg per day. Starting with 100 mg daily for a week, the dosage is gradually increased by 100 mg per week until the desired effect is obtained.

Once the serum uric acid begins to decrease, tissue stores of uric acid become mobilized and there is a risk of their depositing into joints, causing an acute gout attack. Taking colchicine twice a day when starting allopurinol helps prevent these attacks.

Side effects with allopurinol include skin rashes (sometimes severe), nausea, and, rarely, bone marrow suppression or inflammation of the liver.

Probenecid

Probenecid (pro-ben′e-sid) is another medication that is effective in lowering the serum uric acid level. It works by increasing excretion of uric acid by the kidney.

Probenecid comes in 500-mg tablets, with a usual starting dose of one-half tablet, twice a day, for the first week. The dose is gradually increased up to 2000 mg daily or until the serum uric acid returns to normal. Taking colchicine along with the probenecid is advisable for the first six months to prevent an acute attack of gout.

Patients with kidney impairment, or those who produce excessive amounts of uric acid, should receive allopurinol rather than probenecid.

Side effects may include nausea or vomiting, skin rashes, and frequent urination.

Investigational Therapy

Lymph Node Irradiation

Lymph node irradiation is therapy consisting of radiation to certain areas of the body rich in lymph nodes. Radiation reduces the number of circulating T lymphocytes, blood cells that play an important role in the damaging effects of chronic rheumatoid arthritis.

Excessive fatigue and transient low blood count are the most common side effects of this therapy observed so far.

This form of therapy is strictly investigational and is appropriate for only select persons with rheumatoid arthritis who do not respond to conventional therapy.

Plasmapheresis

Plasmapheresis (plaz"muh-ferr'e-sis) is a form of treatment in which a machine removes certain substances from the bloodstream that are causing tissue injury. These substances are usually antibodies and immune complexes.

Plasmapheresis is used only for very serious cases or in life-threatening conditions, such as Goodpasture's syndrome, certain forms of vasculitis, life-threatening SLE, some cases of rheumatoid arthritis, and related conditions. It is not used for the uncomplicated case of rheumatoid arthritis or other forms of common arthritis.

Surgery

Surgery is a very effective form of treatment for some types of arthritis, but it is not for everyone.

Most physicians recommend conservative medical management first, including rest, splints, medications, and hot and cold therapy.

Decisions about surgery should be made after careful consultation with the primary physician and the orthopedic surgeon. The patient may want to seek a second opinion if there are any doubts about the decision.

Pain is the primary reason for surgery, since relief

of pain is the most consistent outcome of reconstructive surgery. Restoration of motion and function is less predictable, and surgery for this reason should be done only after carefully assessing each person's potential improvement.

Many joints may benefit from surgery. The knee is a joint commonly afflicted with arthritis, especially by osteoarthritis and rheumatoid arthritis. There may be progressive loss of movement and increased pain. Surgery may be recommended when pain is present in the joint the majority of the time or when there is difficulty in walking any distance because of limited motion.

The surgical procedure may include arthroscopy, arthroplasty, or synovectomy.

Arthroscopy (ahr-thros'kuh-pee) is a new technique by which the surgeon can look inside the joint with a pencil-sized telescope and determine the extent of damage. Arthroscopy is most commonly used to evaluate the condition of the knee joint but can be used on other joints as well. With arthroscopy, the surgeon can also irrigate the knee to remove loose fragments of tissue, torn cartilage, and diseased synovium that is damaging the joint.

Arthroplasty (ahr'thro-plas"tee) refers to the rebuilding of joints and joint replacement. There have been major advances in replacement of the knee joint. Newer materials and better surgical methods continue to improve the success of joint replacement. Flexibility after knee replacement is generally about 90 degrees of motion.

The hip joint is often a candidate for replacement since arthritis in the hip can cause constant pain and extreme difficulty in walking and sitting. Hip replacement with osteoarthritis now boasts a 95% success rate in the relief of pain and restoration of function. The success rate is nearly as high with rheumatoid arthritis. Hip replacements are now being done in younger people because newer materials have been developed that increase the life of the artificial joint.

Synovectomy (sin"o-veck'tuh-mee), the removal of diseased synovial membrane that causes joint damage, can be done at the wrists and fingers early on to prevent deformity.

The hand and wrist may be extensively affected, especially by rheumatoid arthritis. Deformities can interfere with routine daily functions and lead to embarrassment when the person is unable to perform simple chores.

Inflammation can eventually rupture tendons, especially over the back of the hand, and interfere with the fingers' normal functions. This can be repaired surgically.

If fingers do become deformed, finger joints can be replaced with plastic implants.

There are a variety of other surgical procedures available for joints of the shoulder, elbow, ankle, and foot. Metatarsal resection, for example, is cutting off the ends of bone at the base of the toes. This surgery is performed when pain in this part of the foot prevents walking.

There are many reasons a person should not have surgery for arthritis. The primary reason is that some types of arthritis cannot be helped by surgery.

There are a number of conditions that make surgery inadvisable. With uncontrolled infection, surgery may spread the infection elsewhere in the body. Surgery can be too great a risk for persons with heart and lung disease. Most orthopedic surgeons will not do elective surgery on a knee or hip joint in someone who is significantly overweight. Not only does the excess weight put a strain on the heart, but it also puts undue stress on the operated joint, which interferes with healing and reduces the longevity of an artificial joint.

The period after surgery is as important as the operation itself. Recovery includes rest, exercise, and physical therapy. Following the doctor's instructions is vitally important for a speedy recovery.

The discussion of available drugs has been a bit detailed but nonetheless important to understand. The numerous side effects of the drugs have been described not to frighten you but to make you aware of them so that you will seek medical consultation should they develop. Inform your doctor of side effects as soon as possible. They may not be harmful, but then again you may need to switch medications. Most of these side effects will *not* occur, but it is important to be aware of them so that if they do develop they will cause less concern. You will know that your symptoms are a side effect from a drug and not some new development in your health. It is always less frightening when you know what is happening to your body, and checking with your doctor will give you peace of mind.

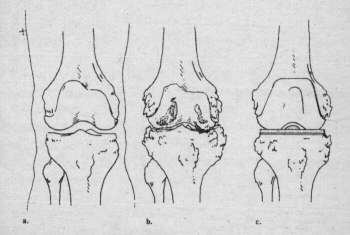

Figure 5.1
(*a*) *Normal knee joint;*
(*b*) *Advanced osteoarthritis of the knee joint;*
(*c*) *Artificial knee joint.*

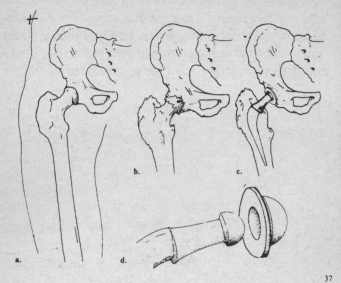

37

Figure 5.2
(a) Normal hip joint;
(b) Advanced osteoarthritis of the hip joint;
(c) Artificial hip joint;
(d) Components of the artificial hip joint.

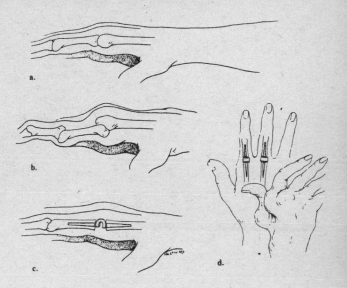

Figure 5.3
(a) *Normal finger joint;*
(b) *Advanced rheumatoid arthritis of the finger joint;*
(c) *Plastic implant in finger joint;*
(d) *Straightening of the fingers following the place-ment of plastic implants in the finger joints.*

6 The Arthritis Family: A Look at the More Notorious Members

Osteoarthritis (OA)

Rheumatoid Arthritis

Systemic Lupus Erythematosus

Gout

Fibrositis

Bursitis

Tendinitis

Back Pain

Ankylosing Spondylitis

Reiter's Syndrome

Psoriatic Arthritis

Juvenile Rheumatoid Arthritis (JRA)

Pseudogout

Infectious Arthritis

Raynaud's Phenomenon

Progressive Systemic Sclerosis (Scleroderma)

Polymyositis and Dermatomyositis

Vasculitis

Polyarteritis Nodosa

Temporal Arteritis

Polymyalgia Rheumatica

Sjogren's Syndrome

ぞぞぞぞ

Now that you know some medical lingo and a bit about medications, it is time to look at the types of arthritis you may have and apply some of this knowledge.

There is a painfully distinct family resemblance among the types of arthritis. There are over one hundred types, but the ones discussed here are the more notorious family members and affect the majority of people.

Some of the drugs and terms previously discussed will be referred to in discussing the particular types of arthritis and the treatment of each.

Osteoarthritis (OA)

Osteoarthritis (os"tee-o-ahr-thrigh'tis) is also referred to as degenerative joint disease. This is the most common type of arthritis, and with age, most people are likely to suffer from osteoarthritis to some degree.

There are at least two kinds of osteoarthritis, often referred to as "primary" and "secondary." Osteoarthritis that develops without any triggering event is the primary kind. Primary osteoarthritis occurs most commonly in women with a positive family history of arthritis. It often affects the small joints of the hands. Secondary osteoarthritis can develop after an injury or repeated strain or in a joint that is previously damaged from another form of arthritis, such as rheumatoid arthritis. It is not uncommon for a person to develop more than one type of arthritis, especially osteoarthritis and rheumatoid arthritis. Secondary osteoarthritis most often affects the larger joints, such as the knees, hips, and spine.

The cause of osteoarthritis is not known, but the damage starts in the cartilage that covers the bones inside the joint (see figure 6.1). Over time the cartilage wears down and loses its smooth contour. Eventually the underlying bones harden and form bony spurs, causing irregular surfaces to rub against each other. Inflammation plays a role, especially following injury or if there is associated deposition of calcium crystals in the joint.

Pain is the most common symptom of osteoarthritis and usually occurs with use of the joint. It is relieved with rest. Swelling, warmth, and stiffness can occur when there is associated inflammation. The afflicted joints may emit creaking or grating sounds called *crepitus* (krep'i-tus) when they are used.

The diagnosis of osteoarthritis is usually made by the physician who takes the history and performs a careful physical exam, especially of the joints. A few laboratory tests, such as a sed rate and rheumatoid factor, may be advised, though the results are usually normal. X rays of the involved joints will show narrowing of the joint space and spurs, the bone's attempt to repair itself. There is not necessarily a good correlation between the severity of the symptoms and the severity of the changes seen on the X rays.

Treatment of osteoarthritis should include a carefully outlined individual plan that aims at reducing pain and discomfort, reducing or preventing disability, and maintaining the individual's independence.

Medications like aspirin and the NSAIDS are especially useful in reducing the pain and, when present, inflammation of osteoarthritis. Unlike rheumatoid arthritis, regular daily doses of the anti-inflammatory drugs are not always necessary with osteoarthritis. Analgesic medications like acetaminophen, when used as needed, may also be effective in controlling the pain.

A balance of rest and exercise is essential for the

treatment of osteoarthritis. Exercise keeps joints moving and strengthens the muscles around the joints, giving the joints support and stability. Rest allows the muscles to relax, but excessive rest makes it harder to move the joints.

Other forms of therapy that may be effective include applying heat or cold to aching joints, soaking in a hot tub, and using devices to reduce chronic pain, such as transcutaneous electrical nerve stimulation (TENS). The TENS consists of a battery-powered box with electrodes attached by adhesive pads over the area of chronic pain. The TENS unit stimulates small nerves under the skin, which reduces the intense pain from the larger, deeper nerve pathways. This is especially helpful for chronic low back pain from osteoarthritis.

Dimethyl sulfoxide (DMSO) (dye-meth'il sulfock'side) is thought by many to benefit various forms of arthritis, including osteoarthritis. DMSO is a chemical by-product of the paper industry, where it is used as a cleaning solvent and an antifreeze agent. The Food and Drug Administration (FDA) has not approved DMSO for use in arthritis. Until its benefit can be shown and its side effects completely understood, its use cannot be recommended.

Surgery, including joint replacement, may be necessary for the hip or knee joint that doesn't respond to conservative therapy.

Rheumatoid Arthritis

Rheumatoid (roo'muh-toyd) arthritis is the most common inflammatory arthritis, affecting nearly 3% of the general population. Rheumatoid arthritis may occur at any age, and three-quarters of those affected are women.

The cause of rheumatoid arthritis is unknown, but recently a specific virus was identified in a small population of rheumatoid patients. This discovery must be confirmed in large numbers of rheumatoid arthritis patients before any definite conclusions can be made. In rheumatoid arthritis, the immune system, which normally defends the body against disease, gets confused and turns against certain parts of the body, especially the joints.

Inflammation plays a major role in rheumatoid arthritis, not only in the joints but possibly in the eyes, lungs, heart, muscles, or nerves. The inflammation starts in the synovium, the thin membrane that lines the joints (see figure 6.1). The synovium becomes very thickened and eventually invades the cartilage and later the bone, possibly causing joint damage. The small joints of the hands and feet, wrists, elbows, shoulders, and knees are the most common joints involved. Symptoms of rheumatoid arthritis usually come on gradually, but in 10% of the cases the onset is abrupt, often occurring overnight in certain persons.

Pain in the joints at rest and with use, prolonged stiffness, especially in the morning, and excessive fatigue are the most common symptoms of rheumatoid arthritis. Loss of appetite, weight loss, and slight fever may also occur.

Diagnosing rheumatoid arthritis may be difficult in the early phases. The history and physical examination often reveal symptoms and signs of inflammation that support the diagnosis. Laboratory tests such as an elevated ESR and a positive blood test for rheumatoid factor further aid a diagnosis of rheumatoid arthritis but are not specific. The rheumatoid factor may be negative in one-third of patients with rheumatoid arthritis. Other blood tests may reveal anemia and other nonspecific elevation of blood proteins.

Early in the disease, X rays of the involved joints are often normal. These X rays serve as a basis for comparison with future X rays to determine the degree of damage.

Treatment programs for rheumatoid arthritis vary from person to person. Most programs include a combination of medications, rest and exercise, heat and cold treatments, joint protection devices, and surgery when advised.

Aspirin and the NSAIDS are the first-line medications in treating rheumatoid arthritis. It is essential to take regular doses of the drugs as prescribed to obtain their maximum effect in reducing inflammation and relieving pain.

Those patients with rheumatoid arthritis that fail to

respond to aspirin or NSAIDS, rest, and heat therapy after an average of six months may require a disease-modifying agent such as hydroxychloroquine or gold compounds. An even smaller percentage of patients that either don't respond to hydroxychloroquine/gold or develop side effects with these medications may require other medications such as D-penicillamine, methotrexate, or azathioprine for control of their arthritis.

Joint protective devices and measures to protect joints are essential to prevent joints from injury and from staying bent. There are self-help devices for everyday activities like bathing, dressing, and eating. A self-help manual is available through the Arthritis Foundation.

Surgery may be necessary for some patients with rheumatoid arthritis. Surgery can correct or prevent deformity, relieve pain, and improve overall movement. The types of surgery available are outlined at the end of chapter 5.

The prognosis (outlook) for rheumatoid arthritis is misunderstood. Many people believe rheumatoid arthritis is a universally crippling disease. At present, with better diagnosis and improved treatment, only 5% or less of those with rheumatoid arthritis develop deformities severe enough to restrict them to bed or a wheelchair.

Spontaneous remissions, periods where the disease goes away on its own, can occur in 20% of people with rheumatoid arthritis. These remissions may last weeks, months, or even years.

With new advances and promising research, there is reason to hope that the cause, and ultimately a cure, for rheumatoid arthritis will be found.

Systemic Lupus Erythematosus

Systemic lupus erythematosus (lew'pus err'i-theem"uh-to'sus) is also referred to as "lupus" or "SLE." The disease affects women about five times more often than men. It usually strikes between ages 20 and 40 but can occur at any age.

Although the cause or causes of SLE remain unknown, the evidence suggests that one's genetic background, female sex hormones (estrogens), and environmental exposures are involved. The role of a viral infection in causing SLE has been looked for but not discovered.

Once the immune system is triggered, it almost becomes an antibody-producing factory. Unfortunately, the antibodies it produces act against itself. These antibodies act against blood cells (platelets, white and red cells), protein, DNA, RNA, and other substances inside the cell.

SLE is characterized by inflammation of many organs. It may occur as a skin rash, fever, joint pain, chest pain, kidney problems, anemia, and even neurologic problems such as seizures. SLE can masquerade in many forms and therefore make it difficult for the physician to make an accurate diagnosis.

The diagnosis of SLE is usually made in the physician's office following the history, physical examination, and several laboratory tests. Many nonspecific lab abnormalities appear with SLE, including anemia, elevated sed rate, low white blood count and platelet count, protein and red blood cells in the urine, and a positive antinuclear antibody (ANA). The ANA, although nonspecific, remains the best screening test for SLE. The physician may also order a DNA antibody test and complement studies to gauge the activity of SLE.

Physicians are now more successful in diagnosing SLE in its early stages, and it is now evident that many more people have a mild form of the disease than previously thought. Many people are under the false impression that a majority of people die of SLE within 10 years. Actually, at present, people who develop SLE have a greater than 90% chance of survival after 10 years of the disease.

Treatment of SLE includes adequate rest and avoiding excessive sun exposure to prevent exacerbations. Contraceptive measures, preferably not oral contraceptives, may be necessary to prevent pregnancy during active phases of the disease, since SLE can get worse during pregnancy and immediately after delivery. This is not to say women with SLE should not get pregnant, but timing the pregnancy to coincide with inactive phases is advisable.

Aspirin and the NSAIDS are effective in reducing the inflammation and controlling the pain in a significant percentage of people. Those who fail to respond to aspirin or NSAIDS, or who develop inflammation of vital organs such as the heart, lung, or kidney, or the nervous system, often require hydroxychloroquine, corticosteroids, or even cytotoxic drugs like azathioprine or cyclophosphamide.

Gout

Unlike some other forms of arthritis, gout (gowt) comes on acutely, even overnight, and the pain is just as immediate and severe.

Gout is due to excessive deposits of uric acid crystals in the joint. Uric acid is a normal substance in the body. Increased amounts of uric acid can be caused by hereditary factors, excessive alcohol, obesity, diuretic pills, or the kidney's inability to rid the body of excess uric acid.

Gout can affect any joint but generally affects those of the leg or foot. The affected joint becomes hot, swollen, and very tender.

Diagnosis of gout may require removing fluid from the affected joint. The fluid is observed under a microscope to check for uric acid crystals. An elevated uric acid in itself is not specific, and a person with an elevated uric acid level will not necessarily develop gout.

Treatment of gout is quite effective. The first phase involves treatment with anti-inflammatory drugs such as colchicine or NSAIDS to relieve the acute pain and inflammation. In the second phase agents such as probenecid or allopurinol are used to lower the uric acid level, if so advisable. Colchicine may be given along with probenecid or allopurinol to help prevent acute gout attacks. In addition to drugs, weight reduction (if the patient is overweight) and limiting alcohol intake are recommended.

Fibrositis

Fibrositis (figh"bro-sigh'tis), also known as fibromyalgia (figh"bro-migh-al'juh) or muscular rheumatism, is one of the most underdiagnosed forms of arthritis. Fibrositis is associated with painful, stiff, and tense muscles and does not directly involve the joints. Because of the pain experienced with movement, the patient may feel as if the joints are involved. The cause of fibrositis is unknown, but stress, physical inactivity, cold, and poor sleep patterns are all aggravating factors. The disorder most commonly affects women in the 30–50 age range.

Fibrositis does not cripple, and it is usually self-limiting. Running its course, the disease may last for weeks, months, or even years, but eventually it will go away on its own. The duration of the disease is as individual as the person.

Diagnosis may be difficult because laboratory tests, X rays, and a physical examination are normal with the exception of painful trigger points. The trigger points are located at the back of the neck, shoulder area, low back, buttocks, elbows, outer hips, and behind the knees. These trigger points are extremely painful to the touch on physical examination of the muscles.

The variability of fibrositis demands open communication with the physician. The doctor knows that the pain is real, but since laboratory tests and the physical examination are normal he or she cannot measure the severity of the discomfort the patient is experiencing. It is up to the patient to inform the doctor about the progression of the disease.

An exercise program is very important in treatment, since inactivity aggravates fibrositis. The program should proceed very gradually from less strenuous exercise to more strenuous, because the patient will find exercising painful. Aspirin or NSAIDs may be used to relieve pain, and muscle relaxants or tricyclic medications may also be necessary if the person experiences disturbed sleep patterns.

Bursitis

Although often confused with arthritis of the joint, bursitis (bur-sigh′tis) is inflammation of the bursa surrounding the joints. A bursa is a sac of lubricating fluid that allows tendons and muscles to move around the joint. Bursitis most commonly affects the shoulders, elbows, and hips. There may be significant swelling and redness of the bursa, which explains why it is confused with arthritis of the joint. The physician can diagnose bursitis on physical examination, localizing points of tenderness outside the joint. Results of lab tests are usually normal.

Treatment usually includes anti-inflammatory drugs or injections of cortisone into the site.

Tendinitis

Also confused with arthritis of a joint, tendinitis (ten"duh-nigh'tis) (or tendonitis) is inflammation of a tendon from a muscle. Moving the muscle causes pain. The physician diagnoses tendinitis, finding pain by examining the tendon outside the joint. Treatment of tendinitis involves heat packs, rest, drugs to relieve pain and inflammation, and sometimes injections of cortisone into the site.

Back Pain

Back pain is a common symptom of many different types of arthritis, but arthritis is not the only cause of back pain. Injuries, posture problems, lack of exercise, emotional upset, and congenital malformations of the spine can all cause back pain.

Pain in the back can originate from the vertebrae (the bone structure of the spine), muscles, ligaments, discs (the cushions between vertebrae), and nerves. Common problems that cause back pain include lack of exercise and obesity, which stresses the muscles that are essential in supporting the spine. Injuries from accidents, athletics, and awkward motion during routine activities can all injure ligaments, muscles, or discs.

Osteoarthritis is the most common form of arthritis that causes chronic low back pain. Spurs and disc degeneration from osteoarthritis can compress the muscles or nerves as they exit the spinal canal. Other forms of arthritis that cause low back pain are ankylosing spondylitis, some cases of Reiter's syndrome and psoriatic arthritis, fibrositis, polymyalgia rheumatica, and rheumatoid arthritis.

Back pain is either acute or chronic. Acute back pain is most common. Almost everyone experiences short twinges or muscle spasms that come on suddenly and last for seconds, hours, or even days. The great majority of cases of acute low back pain resolve without specific treatment.

Chronic low back pain can be quite disabling. Chronic pain often breeds stress and anxiety, and these often make the chronic pain worse.

The evaluation and diagnosis of back pain includes a history and physical examination by the physician.

If the back pain has been present for only a few days and not precipitated by an injury, X rays and laboratory testing are often not necessary. On the other hand, evaluating chronic low back pain is aided by X rays and laboratory testing. Unless there is a primary abnormality in the bone itself, the X rays are often normal. Ligamentous sprain, muscular strain, or ruptured discs do not show up on plain X rays. If the symptoms associated with the back pain suggest pressure on a nerve or the spinal cord, more sophisiticated testing such as computerized axial tomography (CAT scan) or a myelogram may be advisable.

Fortunately, most cases of back pain get better on their own. Once an accurate diagnosis is made, recommended treatment may include rest, hot and cold therapy, proper posture and shoes, and a careful exercise program. Depending on the severity and cause of the back pain, helpful medications include muscle relaxants, aspirin and NSAIDS, and acetaminophen. More severe cases often require codeine or propoxyphene. The TENS unit and relaxation therapy can help control chronic pain without adverse effects.

Surgery and nerve blocks have an important place in the management of back pain. Consultation by an orthopedic surgeon or neurosurgeon is advised if the physician believes surgery might be necessary. Significant advances have been made in controlling chronic back pain with nerve blocks. These are often done by anesthesiologists or other pain specialists.

Ankylosing Spondylitis

Ankylosing spondylitis (ank'i-loaz-ing spon"di-lye'tis) is an inflammatory arthritis most commonly affecting the spine, hips, knees, and ankles.

The cause is unknown, but progress has been made in finding the cause by the identification of a genetic marker called HLA-B-27. This marker is found in 90% of patients with ankylosing spondylitis. About 8% of the general population have this B-27 marker. It is thought that the presence of this marker somehow predisposes the person to develop ankylosing spondylitis and several other noted disorders, such as Reiter's syndrome and psoriatic spondylitis.

Ankylosing spondylitis affects men and women equally, though men tend to have more symptoms. Women tend to have a milder form of the disease and one that more frequently involves peripheral (hip, knee) joints.

Low back pain and stiffness are the most common symptoms. The symptoms come and go, while the stiffness often gets better with exercise. The course of the disease varies, but often it progresses slowly, eventually leading to fusion of the spine and loss of flexibility.

Ankylosing spondylitis is diagnosed after a medical history, physical examination, X rays, and lab studies. In the early stages of the disease, X rays of the back will be normal. Later, there is disruption of the sacroiliac joints. The lab tests may show an elevated sed rate, mild anemia, and a negative rheumatoid factor. Checking for the presence of the HLA-B-27 genetic marker is not necessary in the majority of cases. While this marker is present in 90% of ankylosing spondylitis cases, it is an expensive test that can be avoided, since other methods of diagnosing are usually reliable.

Treatment of ankylosing spondylitis is most dependent on good posture, regular exercise, and drugs to relieve inflammation. People with ankylosing spondylitis respond better to NSAIDS than aspirin, but aspirin is less expensive and can be tried first.

Reiter's Syndrome

Reiter's (right'erz) syndrome is an inflammatory arthritis that usually affects the leg joints, such as those at the knee, heel, or ankle. People with Reiter's syndrome can have arthritis of the spine, similar to ankylosing spondylitis. There may also be inflammation of the eye (conjunctivitis, iritis), inflammation of the urethra (urethritis), and in severe cases a skin rash.

Young men, ages 20 to 40, are the most common victims, but women can also get the disease. The cause is unknown, but Reiter's syndrome can come on after certain infections of the bowel or urethra. The majority of patients with Reiter's syndrome have the genetic marker HLA-B-27.

The diagnosis of Reiter's syndrome is made after a

history, a physical examination, and laboratory tests. There is not a specific test for diagnosing Reiter's syndrome, but the sed rate is usually elevated, the rheumatoid factor is negative, and there may be mild anemia.

The prognosis of Reiter's syndrome is variable. It was once thought that in the majority of patients the disease would have a self-limited course. It is now apparent that most people will have chronic, recurrent joint symptoms of pain and swelling.

Reiter's syndrome is treated with drugs to reduce pain and inflammation. Patients with Reiter's syndrome will respond better to NSAIDS than aspirin. Rarely, a severe case may require cytotoxic agents.

Psoriatic Arthritis

Psoriasis (so-rye'uh-sis) is a common disease that affects the skin. The scalp, elbows, knees, and body creases are most commonly affected with psoriasis.

Only about one in five people suffering from psoriasis will develop arthritis. Five different forms of arthritis can occur. In the most common form several joints are involved, such as a few fingers, toes, or a knee. Other forms include involvement of joints at the tips of fingers, involvement of multiple joints (identical to rheumatoid arthritis), inflammation of the spine (spondylitis), and arthritis multilans, which is the most destructive and fortunately the least common. In 80%

of people with psoriatic arthritis, the psoriasis causes pitting or elevation of the nails.

The diagnosis of psoriatic arthritis is made after a careful history and physical examination and a few laboratory tests. The rheumatoid factor is usually negative and the sed rate is often elevated. X rays of the involved joints may also be helpful.

The prognosis of psoriatic arthritis is good in that most people will have a mild and limited form of the disease. Because it is a chronic form of arthritis, the symptoms may come and go. Occasionally psoriatic arthritis is crippling.

Treatment of psoriatic arthritis includes adequate rest and localized therapy, such as heat packs. Drugs, such as the NSAIDS, are useful to relieve pain and inflammation. In general, patients respond better to the NSAIDS than aspirin. Gold and methotrexate may be necessary in severe cases. In cases of generalized skin disease, medical treatment to improve the skin disease may also improve the arthritis.

Juvenile Rheumatoid Arthritis (JRA)

Between 60,000 and 200,000 children suffer from JRA. Forms of arthritis that affect children include SLE, ankylosing spondylitis, dermatomyositis, and others that are much less common.

The consequences of JRA may include growth retardation, inflammation of the eyes (iritis), and enlargement of the spleen and lymph nodes.

Girls are affected more often than boys, but the ratio varies with age and presentation.

JRA manifests itself in many different forms. Often the first sign of JRA is a child limping because of limited motion of a knee or an ankle. Severe pain or pain at rest is unusual, in contrast to adult rheumatoid arthritis. Other forms of JRA include multiple joint involvement that mimics adult rheumatoid or systemic illness with high fever, skin rash, and muscle and joint complaints. One form affecting boys over 10 years of age involves a few joints, is associated with HLA-B-27, and often develops into ankylosing spondylitis in adulthood.

Diagnosing JRA is often difficult at first. Many other conditions need to be excluded. The laboratory tests usually reveal anemia, an elevated sedimentation rate, and a negative rheumatoid factor. X rays of the involved joints most often are normal.

The overall outlook for JRA is favorable. Seventy-five to ninety percent of children with JRA have a good prognosis, with no symptoms or only mild ones and little or no deformity.

Treatment of JRA is aimed at relief of symptoms of active disease and maintenance of joint position, function, and muscle strength. Physical treatments of JRA are as important as medications.

The first drug of choice to reduce inflammation is

aspirin. The dose of aspirin is adjusted to the weight of the child in kilograms. Aspirin is the only drug necessary in the majority of children with JRA. Reye's syndrome, resulting in liver damage, rarely occurs in children with JRA on a high dose of aspirin. The risk of Reye's syndrome is increased if the child has chicken pox or flu illness (influenza), in which case aspirin should be temporarily stopped and the physician contacted.

A small percentage of children with JRA who do not respond to aspirin, NSAIDS, or rest and physical therapy may require gold compounds to control their disease.

Regular eye examinations by an ophthalmologist are necessary to detect early inflammation of the eyes (iritis), since it often occurs without symptoms and yet is very treatable.

Finally, regular conferences with the physician, family members, and teachers are essential.

Pseudogout

Pseudogout (sue"do-gowt') is caused by calcium crystal deposition into joints. The condition can take many forms and be confused with gout, rheumatoid arthritis, and osteoarthritis.

Pseudogout most commonly affects people over the age of 50 and most commonly affects the knee. It can manifest as an acutely painful joint, as in gout, or it may act like a more chronic inflammatory arthritis involving many joints, like rheumatoid arthritis. Many people with osteoarthritis have incidental calcium crystals in their joints that may never cause any acute symptoms.

Diagnosis of pseudogout depends on the presence of calcium crystals in synovial fluid removed from an involved joint. Pseudogout may be suspected when X rays demonstrate calcification of cartilage in the joint.

Pseudogout is treated with drugs to relieve pain and inflammation. Injection of corticosteroids into a joint may also be quite beneficial in some cases.

Infectious Arthritis

Infectious arthritis is a disorder caused by a direct invasion of an organism, such as bacteria, viruses, and fungi, that cause infection.

Bacteria are the most common organisms. These include bacteria that cause gonorrhea and staphylococcus organisms. Common viruses causing infection are the hepatitis virus and a virus that causes German measles.

Infectious arthritis usually comes on suddenly and may involve any joint. People with underlying illnesses, such as chronic alcoholism, drug abuse, diabetes, or cancer, have increased risk of infection. People with previously damaged joints, such as from rheumatoid arthritis, also have an increased risk.

Infectious arthritis requires prompt diagnosis and treatment. The diagnosis is made by identifying the organism causing the infection. Treatment includes the appropriate antibiotic and resting the involved joint. With effective treatment, there is usually no damage to the joints.

Raynaud's Phenomenon

Raynaud's (ray-noz') phenomenon occurs with cold exposure. The color of the skin changes from white to blue to red. One needs only two of the three phases to have Raynaud's.

Raynaud's is quite common, and especially affects young women 20 to 40 years old. Many people will have Raynaud's for many years and not develop any other condition, but some may develop another form of arthritis, especially scleroderma and sometimes systemic lupus erythematosus (SLE).

The diagnosis of Raynaud's is made after the history and physical examination. Provocative testing, such as placing the hands in ice water, is not advisable and may be dangerous. The lab tests often performed that may result as abnormal are antinuclear antibody, blood count, sed rate, rheumatoid factor, and cryoglobulins.

The treatment is based on protecting the fingers and hands from the cold, such as wearing gloves in cold weather as well as when using the freezer or refrigerator. When Raynaud's appears with symptoms of burning, tingling fingertips, or ulcers on the tips of the fingers, medication may be necessary. Drugs that improve circulation by relaxing the blood vessels are helpful and include prazosin (Minipress), Dibenzyline, nifedipine (Procardia), diltiazem (Cardizem), and verapamil (Calan, Isoptin). In rare cases surgery, such as sympathectomy, is necessary. A sympathectomy involves cutting the nerves that cause the blood vessels to narrow, decreasing blood supply. Injecting a drug called reserpine into the artery of the involved extremity can reduce the spasm and may help heal the ulcers on the fingers or toes.

Progressive Systemic Sclerosis (Scleroderma)

Scleroderma (skleer"o-dur'muh) means hard skin, which characterizes progressive systemic sclerosis. People with scleroderma have tight, bound-down skin, most commonly of the fingers and face.

Although the exact cause of scleroderma is unknown, damage to very small blood vessels eventually decreases the blood flow to the skin and organs of the body, causing progressive scarring. The scarring in scleroderma is the body's normal scarring reaction, though abnormal in location, amount, and persistence.

Most people with scleroderma have Raynaud's phenomenon. Hardening of the skin is characteristic and initially may be confined to the fingers. In early phases before hardening of the skin, there may be swelling of the fingers, called the edema phase. Later the swelling goes away, leaving taut, hard skin.

Any organ can be involved with the scleroderma process, but the gastrointestinal tract, especially the esophagus, is the most common. Scleroderma affecting the esophagus can lead to heartburn or difficulty in swallowing. The small and large intestines may also be involved, causing dilatation or outpouchings. Scarring of the kidney leads to severe elevations of blood pressure and may alter the kidney's ability to filter waste products. Scarring of the lungs and heart can also occur, causing shortness of breath or abnormalities of the heart rhythm.

The diagnosis of scleroderma is often made by observing characteristic skin changes. Most laboratory tests do not show specific abnormalities for scleroderma. In making a diagnosis a skin biopsy is sometimes done, and X ray studies, especially barium studies of the gastrointestinal tract, may show characteristic findings.

Scleroderma (progressive systemic sclerosis) is not necessarily progressive. Most people will suffer during an active period that varies in length but often lasts several years. During this time, the skin that is affected is usually limited to the face, fingers, neck, and forearms. It is uncommon for the scleroderma to affect all of the skin.

The most serious complication of scleroderma is kidney involvement, which occurs in about 10% of people. Warning signs of kidney involvement include severe headaches, marked elevation of blood pressure, or visual difficulty. Severe kidney involvement can lead to death if not treated early. Improved blood pressure control, dialysis, and kidney transplantation has improved the prognosis.

The treatment of scleroderma centers more around the patient than specific drug therapy. To date there is no cure, nor is there any uniformly effective therapy that alters the scleroderma process. There are a few reports of improvement with D-penicillamine. Chlorambucil (klor-am'bew-sil), a drug of the cytotoxic class, is also being used on an investigational basis to slow the scleroderma process. Skin care is essential, keeping the fingers and hands as mobile as possible. In addition, because of the associated Raynaud's phenomenon, keeping the fingers warm with gloves and protecting the hands from cold may prevent damage to fingertips.

If heartburn develops, antacids or medicines that reduce acid secretion, such as cimetidine (sim"i-tigh'deen) (Tagamet) or ranitidine (ran"i-tigh'deen) (Zantac), may be useful in preventing complications later. Metoclopramide (met"o-klo-pram'ide) (Reglan) is a useful drug that stimulates the muscles of the esophagus and stomach, which reduces the symptoms of regurgitation of stomach acid into the esophagus. If muscle inflammation develops, corticosteroids may be necessary. Finally, if the kidney becomes involved, controlling blood pressure with medications is essential, as well as close medical supervision.

Polymyositis and Dermatomyositis

Polymyositis (pol"ee-migh-o-sigh'tis) and dermatomyositis (dur"muh-toe-migh-o-sigh'tis) are conditions characterized by inflammation of muscles. This inflammation may lead to pain, weakness, and destruction of the muscles.

The cause is unknown, but for some reason the person's blood cells, called lymphocytes, become sensitized to the body's muscles and attack the muscles, leading to uncontrolled inflammation.

The skin may also be involved. If so, the condition is called dermatomyositis. Symptoms of skin involvement include a violaceous color over the eyelids and knuckles. A red rash may be seen over the chest and face.

Muscle weakness is the most common symptom. Although any muscle can be involved, those muscles of the upper arms and legs are most commonly affected. The weakness may manifest itself in difficulty in brushing your hair, inability to get out of the bathtub or a deep chair, or trouble swallowing liquid or food. There may be involvement of the lungs, such as from scar tissue or from aspiration of contents that are not adequately swallowed.

Polymyositis or dermatomyositis are sometimes associated with underlying cancer. About 15% of adults with polymyositis and dermatomyositis may have cancer. Childhood dermatomyositis is not associated with cancer.

The diagnosis is made after detecting abnormal muscle weakness, elevation of muscle enzymes (CPK, SGOT, and aldolase), abnormal muscle biopsy that reveals muscle cell damage and inflammation, and an abnormal electromyogram (EMG) that shows irritation of the muscle. The EMG tests the muscles and nerves by measuring the activity of small needles placed in the muscles. The EMG is a great help in diagnosing diseases affecting the muscles and nerves.

The prognosis of polymyositis or dermatomyositis depends on the severity of muscle weakness and on whether the lungs are involved. Some people may require ventilatory support if muscles of the chest wall or the lungs have been damaged by the disease. Older people, and those with associated cancer, have a less favorable prognosis. Those with a milder form of the disease will do well for many years.

Polymyositis and dermatomyositis are treated with corticosteroids in the form of prednisone. Prednisone is given for an extended time, since improving muscle strength and returning muscle enzymes to normal takes weeks to months.

Those who do not respond to prednisone may require treatment with methotrexate or azathioprine (Imuran).

Recovery is slow with polymyositis and dermato-myositis. Continued activity to strengthen and improve muscle function is necessary.

Vasculitis

Vasculitis (vas"kew-lye'tis) is a general term that refers to inflammation and destruction of blood vessels, such as arteries or veins. The list of disorders associated with vasculitis is extensive.

The cause of most forms of vasculitis is unknown, but researchers have discovered a relationship between hepatitis-B virus and some forms of vasculitis. Most cases of vasculitis are associated with deposition of immune complexes.

Polyarteritis nodosa was the first form of vasculitis to be identified. Since then, a number of infections, including bacteria and viral infections, drugs like penicillin and sulfas, and many different forms of arthritis, such as rheumatoid arthritis or SLE, have been associated with vasculitis.

The features of vasculitis can include skin rashes, large bruises over the legs, stomach pain, generalized muscle and joint aches, infiltration of the lungs, blood in the urine, neurologic disorders, unexplained fever, and weight loss. A combination of several of these features in the same patient should make one suspect vasculitis.

The diagnosis is made by identifying any possible cause, such as an infection, drug, or underlying arthritis. A specific tissue biopsy of skin, muscle, nerve, or kidney may be necessary for a positive diagnosis.

Treatment of vasculitis depends on the cause, and on whether there is a threat of damage to a vital organ. If infection is present, it should be treated; if it is caused by a drug, the drug should be stopped. If the vasculitis is damaging organs, drugs such as corticosteroids and cytotoxic agents can reduce inflammation and reduce antibody formation.

Polyarteritis Nodosa

Polyarteritis nodosa (pol"ee-ahr"te-rye′tis no-do′suh) was the first form discovered of the general disorder now called vasculitis.

Polyarteritis is an uncommon condition that occurs in middle-aged people. The features are variable and can include unexplained fever, weight loss, abdominal pain, elevation of blood pressure, with blood cells in the urine, generalized muscle and joint aches, and even neurologic problems, such as inability to lift the foot or hand.

The diagnosis of polyarteritis is difficult. The laboratory abnormalities are nonspecific but may include an elevated ESR (sed rate) and anemia on blood count. The physician may need to biopsy an organ, such as the kidney, or a muscle or nerve in order to make the diagnosis. An angiogram, which is an X ray of the blood vessels after they have been injected with dye, may be necessary for diagnosis.

Treatment involves a combination of a corticosteroid medication, such as prednisone, and a cytotoxic drug, like cyclophosphamide (Cytoxan). These are very powerful immune suppressive drugs and must be monitored very carefully by your physician. The treatment is continued for many months and often for several years.

Fortunately, the prognosis of polyarteritis is much improved by early diagnosis and with the treatment outlined above.

Temporal Arteritis

Temporal arteritis (tem'puh-rul ahr"te-rye'tis) is one of the common forms of vasculitis. It affects people over the age of 50, the average age at which it strikes being 70.

Although temporal arteritis is related to polymyalgia rheumatica, a person can suffer from both disorders, or each one separately.

The symptoms of temporal arteritis may include severe headaches, visual difficulty, such as double vision or blurred vision, fever, weight loss, and even serious depression and apathy. When temporal arteritis is associated with fleeting loss of vision, there is a risk of blindness and an urgent need for medical attention.

Laboratory tests can be helpful in diagnosis. An elevated sed rate in the range of 50–100 mm/hr is evidence of temporal arteritis. Other lab abnormalities include anemia and nonspecific elevation of liver function tests.

Because of the many different clinical manifestations of temporal arteritis, the physician must have a high degree of suspicion to make an early diagnosis. A temporal artery biopsy is often needed for a positive diagnosis. Not all people will require a biopsy, nor will the biopsy be positive in 100% of the cases, but a vast majority of people with temporal arteritis will have a positive temporal artery biopsy.

Treatment is very effective when temporal arteritis is diagnosed early. Most commonly, treated with prednisone (60–80 mg per day), the patient shows a positive response within 24 hours. The dose of prednisone is gradually reduced over a period of months, while the level of the sed rate is monitored. Duration of treatment varies, but usually is at least one year.

Polymyalgia Rheumatica

Polymyalgia rheumatica (pol"ee-migh-al'jee-uh roomat'i-kuh) is a disorder commonly affecting people over the age of 50. Polymyalgia means "many painful muscles."

The cause of polymyalgia rheumatica is unknown, but because of its relationship to temporal arteritis it may be caused by vasculitis.

People suffering from polymyalgia rheumatica complain of severe aching and stiffness of the neck, shoulder, and hip muscles. There is not usually weakness with the disease, but weakness can develop since people may not use the muscles because of pain. Other possible symptoms are low-grade fever, weight loss, and generalized fatigue. These symptoms can be confused with those of cancer.

If a patient with polymyalgia has associated inflammation of large blood vessels (vasculitis), especially of the head, the condition is called giant cell arteritis (temporal arteritis). Temporal arteritis causes severe headache, blurred vision, and, less commonly, blindness.

The diagnosis is made after a careful history and physical examination and finding the following abnormal laboratory test results: markedly elevated sed rate, anemia measured on the blood count, and when applicable a temporal artery biopsy revealing severe destruction and inflammation of the blood vessel.

The good news about polymyalgia is that when an accurate diagnosis is made, treatment is dramatically effective. The treatment consists of corticosteroid medication such as prednisone. The dosage depends on whether there is associated temporal arteritis. Improvement usually occurs within 24 hours. A person can be nearly bedridden one day and the following day, after proper treatment, be ready to run down the hall.

The duration of treatment varies but averages about

a year. Your physician will monitor the ESR (sed rate) and gradually decrease the dose of prednisone.

Sjogren's Syndrome

Sjogren's (show'grens) syndrome is an autoimmune condition characterized by chronic inflammation of the salivary and lacrimal (tear producing) glands. This inflammation gradually damages these glands, causing a decreased production of saliva and tears that results in dry eyes and mouth.

Sjogren's can occur as a "primary" condition, without any other type of arthritis, or as a "secondary" condition, most commonly associated with rheumatoid arthritis. Ten to fifteen percent of people with rheumatoid arthritis will have Sjogren's syndrome. It may also occur with SLE, progressive systemic sclerosis (scleroderma), or polymyositis.

The most common symptoms are a sandy or gritty or burning sensation in the eyes and a dry mouth causing difficulty in chewing and swallowing. The excessive dryness often leads to frequent dental caries (cavities) and may cause small sores on the cornea of the eye. Enlargement of salivary glands, such as the parotid gland in front of the mandible, is common.

Sjogren's syndrome may be associated with other autoimmune conditions affecting the body, including thyroid disorders, neurologic conditions, conditions of the stomach and bowel, and diseases affecting the hormone glands.

The diagnosis of Sjogren's syndrome is made by demonstration of decreased tear production or by a lip biopsy that reveals damage to the glands. Laboratory tests may reveal an elevated sed rate, anemia, positive rheumatoid factor or antinuclear antibody (ANA), elevated serum proteins, and other antibodies to cell substances.

Treatment of Sjogren's syndrome is symptomatic and includes using artificial tears, drinking frequent liquids, and intermittent evaluations by the eye doctor (ophthalmologist). Corticosteroids, NSAIDs, or cytotoxic drugs occasionally are advisable if more serious organ involvement occurs.

Though personalities differ, types of arthritis have one common family trait—they are pains in the neck, as well as in virtually every other part of the body. Arthritis is not something you choose to have, and you don't have any say about what type you will get. What you can control, to some degree, is how arthritis will affect your life. A doctor will diagnose the exact type that has come to live with you and then prescribe the course of action to deal with it.

Congratulations! You have just completed Phase One of your responsibility—an Education. You have learned some information that will enable you to talk to your doctor. Perhaps some questions occurred to you as you read the sections pertinent to you. Write them down, and the next time you visit your doctor, ask!

Most of the education section concerned necessary treatment of the symptoms of arthritis. But what about patient responsibility and taking care of the whole person? Move on to Phase Two of your responsibility— Taking Control of Arthritis.

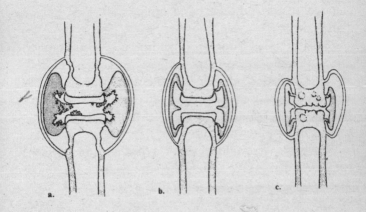

Figure 6.1
(a) Joint showing active rheumatoid arthritis, characterized by thickened synovial lining and bone erosions;
(b) Normal joint;
(c) Joint showing advanced osteoarthritis, characterized by loss of cartilage and thickening of the bone.

PHASE TWO

422422

Taking Control
of Arthritis

Gaining control over arthritis will not happen overnight. More than likely you did not lose control overnight, and gaining control may take some time. You've already started by learning about arthritis in the previous chapters—this is your ammunition to begin the battle. To be prepared for the battle means working out physically and mentally.

There seems to be a fitness revolution going on in America. Just because you have arthritis, you don't have to be left out. You can still exercise, eat well, and strive to be as healthy as you possibly can. You have a new scale, and you won't be as healthy as you would without arthritis. But maybe you didn't take care of yourself before you got arthritis. If that is the case, taking care of yourself now may produce a pleasant surprise— you may feel better than ever.

Taking control mentally means developing a positive attitude. Developing a good attitude involves exercising the mind, which may be more difficult than physical exercise. There are exercises to develop the mind and the body, and the bonus is that they sometimes overlap. If you want to be healthy, both mentally and physically, the benefits far outweigh the work involved.

You can achieve the highest degree of health on your scale—the spectrum of health within a chronic disease—with a little work and a lot of determination. It will help your arthritis and get you in control.

7 Stress and Arthritis

Learn to Relax

Develop a Routine

Develop a Positive Attitude

Learn to Pick and Choose Your Stress

ટ્ટેટ્ટેટ્ટેટ્ટે

There are those who believe that arthritis can be brought on by stress. Stress certainly aggravates arthritis, and it is important to avoid undue stress. Comparing stress and arthritis produces some interesting ideas. Remember that inflammation in itself is not bad. Inflammation is a reaction to an injury. Inflammation out of control, however, is arthritis. Stress is like that. Stress is not all bad, because the absence of stress means that nothing is being accomplished. Your body undergoes a chemical reaction to prepare it when it feels threatened. This is very important, but if the body is ready to fight constantly, then stress too becomes uncontrolled and can be harmful. Both stress and arthritis (inflammation) are good until they are out of control. Then they become harmful.

Like inflammation, stress can be a reaction to physical injury. When you are threatened or in an emergency situation, stress acts as a defense mechanism to ready you for the fight. Because arthritis is an injury to the body, your body is under a stress alert. Ironically, arthritis causes stress and stress aggravates arthritis. Your body is caught up in a vicious cycle: stress aggravates arthritis, arthritis aggravates stress...

But as in the old chicken and the egg phenomenon, the origin doesn't really matter. Because your body is handling all of this internal stress, it becomes more important for you to avoid external stress. Remember, some stresses are important, so you must learn to distinguish the difference. You need to ask yourself a couple of questions before you react to a situation. *How* you react, not the situation itself, will cause stress.

First of all, "Am I in physical danger?" If you are being attacked or are involved in a car accident or in any number of cases, the answer will be yes. These are necessary stresses and your body will deal with them before you have much chance to think about it. These types of stresses, thank goodness, do not occur constantly. What can occur constantly and what you do have control over is less important stress. Nonetheless, it is just as dangerous if it puts your body on red alert. Ask yourself this question, "Will this situation (or my reaction to it) ultimately change my life?" If so, how?

If you are five minutes late for work, it is probably not going to affect your life. So calm down, relax, and think, "I'll get there when I get there." Getting excited, frustrated, and driving fast causes undue stress. However, if you are late frequently, and your boss specifically told you that you will be fired if you are late again, then obviously that does affect your life and is due stress. That is a whole new problem, and you need to rid yourself of that stress by getting up earlier, organizing better the night before, or doing whatever it takes to solve your time problem.

It makes sense then to reduce stress, but how? There are as many answers to that as there are people and situations. It is purely individual, but there are some general guidelines that can help.

Learn to Relax

Relaxation can be achieved by several methods. One method involves being aware of various parts of your body. As a kid, you may have talked to your toes. You aren't going to do that as an adult. (If you do, don't tell anyone about it—your toes won't.) But the idea is simply to be aware of your toes. You may have heard of a technique that helps in falling asleep. Visualize your toes in your mind and concentrate until they relax. Move on to the feet, ankles, calves, and repeat the procedure up the body, until the entire body is relaxed. This works if you don't cheat, that is, if you truly concentrate on a specific body part and not two million other things. It is not easy and may take some practice. After all, it does seem a bit silly to forget about mortgage payments, deadlines, sick children, and the like, just to think about ten funny looking things at the end of your feet. But if it works, do it. If not, find another method of relaxation that does work.

This type of visualization can be effective if practiced and can evolve into more imaginative images than toes. For instance, people with Raynaud's can actually raise the temperature of their hands by concentrating and visualizing that they are holding something warm, or that their hands are submerged in warm water.

If your knee seems to be throbbing as if it is being hit by a hammer, visualize a hammer hitting your knee. If you can visualize it pounding, visualize it slowly running out of steam, hitting less frequently until it stops.

Visualization exercises are not for everyone, but they can work if you make a real effort, truly concentrate, and practice the skills. The only limiting factor of this technique is your imagination.

Another method of relaxation is deep breathing. When you are overly excited or agitated, you may begin breathing deeply without thinking. Excessive deep breathing can cause hyperventilation, so you must learn to think about breathing. Being aware of and controlling breathing can have a calming and relaxing effect. Incorporate some visualization and concentrate on an object or body part as you slowly inhale and exhale.

Breathing exercises are a bonus for people with arthritis because while they are relaxing they can also ease pain. When you are in pain you tense up, and tension can aggravate pain. As you breathe and relax, pain is alleviated. Remember when we talked about childbirth earlier in the book? The idea behind natural childbirth is to use breathing to reduce pain. The mother is instructed to concentrate on an object, a focal point. As contractions come, she is to inhale slowly through her nose and exhale slowly through her mouth. This technique changes as labor progresses, but the point is to try to think about something else, to get her mind off the immediate pain.

The principle is basically the same for relaxation. Instead of involuntarily breathing deeply in a stressful situation, think about it. Close your eyes, visualize something, perhaps a body part that seems to be particularly tense. Inhale slowly through your nose until you cannot take in any more air. Hold it briefly, and then exhale slowly through your mouth. Repeat a couple of times, then breathe normally.

Believe it or not, exercise can also help you relax. You can incorporate your breathing and visualization skills while exercising and kill two birds with one stone. Chapter 8 discusses the benefits of exercise in detail and illustrates various exercises. But as a rule of thumb, to incorporate breathing with exercise, inhale when you contract or tighten a muscle, exhale as you relax the muscle.

Relaxation is not something to do once in a while. You are hit by stress constantly and there is no set schedule. For this reason, you need to use relaxation skills to deal with stress as it occurs. Your body is a very good indicator of when you need to relax. Suddenly, you are aware that you are clinching your teeth. Stop, concentrate on your jaw and mouth. Let your jaw drop and relax your facial muscles. Do some deep breathing. Use this procedure anytime you become aware of tension. Vary the procedure to suit the body part. If it is your back, do some stretching; if it is your neck, rotate your head, and so on. The point is to relax on a small scale, frequently, to avoid relaxing on a large scale and be stuck in bed.

One final word about relaxation—learn to wait. If you have to wait in line or wait for someone at a restaurant, and you don't really have to be anywhere else, don't get irritable. See waiting as an opportunity to spend time on yourself. Daydream, think, plan, or just people watch. Realize that it was ten or however many minutes of unexpected, unplanned time that you get to spend with someone you really like—you!

Develop a Routine

Routine and dullness are not synonymous. Routine has a bad reputation in this country, and people are made to feel guilty for being in a rut. If you happen to be happy with your rut, dig in and hold on to it. Routine can be important in making you feel in control, that things are in order and that you are in charge of those things. If making the bed each morning establishes a sense of order, then do it. The fact that someone else thinks making a bed is useless shouldn't bother you. They probably have a different ritual that seems useless to you.

Your routine should include a time called, "Watch a Soap." This can be taken literally or not. You can actually pick a soap opera and at a designated time each day lie down, rest, and watch. More likely though it will be a specific time that you set aside as a diversion, a time that requires little if any physical or mental energy from you. The soap is a good example, because you know that it airs at a certain time. If your work is not done and you work beyond that time, you've missed it, it's over. By the same token, if you work through your diversion time, it's over too. Time does not wait. If you miss "your time," it's gone. If you miss "your time" everyday, you will become frustrated and feel stress.

You will miss days of course, but take those in stride. Short-term stress is not really harmful in the long haul. If you can have "your time" most of the time, stress will not be a problem.

Be reasonable about the amount, too. Let's face it, if you watch five soaps a day, you are not accomplishing much with your life.

Develop a routine. Organize your time to include a daily (or nearly daily) diversion time. Routine will give you a sense of power over daily events, put you in control. Besides, establishing a routine makes breaking it every once in a while more exciting.

Develop a Positive Attitude

Attitude plays a very important role in reducing stress. You feel stress because of *how* you react to a situation not because of the situation itself. Therefore, how you react depends on your attitude. A positive attitude can reduce stress. There is no magic formula for creating a positive attitude. It cannot be taught. It comes from within you, and it may require some effort. If you have arthritis, the payoff is too great not to try.

If you were an optimist before arthritis, you will have a fight on your hands. If you were a pessimist to begin with, you will probably take on all the negative aspects of arthritis. If you notice those negative characteristics developing—irritability, complaining, self-centeredness, apathy, defeatism—you surely will not want them as parts of your personality. If you want to fight these tendencies, you've taken the first step toward a positive attitude.

Do not give arthritis too much credit. You do not have a neon sign imprinted in your forehead that blinks "arthritic." You have many interests and qualities that have nothing to do with arthritis. My aunt has a saying, "I will probably die of cancer while treating my arthritis." This somewhat humorous statement reveals a lot. You may overlook other medical problems, attributing all symptoms to arthritis. People with arthritis do get colds, flu, and other diseases. You may also blame arthritis for every disappointment and failure. This kind of thinking not only promotes a negative attitude, it can be medically dangerous as well. Arthritis doesn't deserve so much of your attention.

Family members and friends can help you with your attitude. Positive begets positive, and negative begets negative. If you complain all the time, others will encourage it. If you roll your eyes and moan, "I feel so awful," others are likely to agree with you and say, "Yes, you really look bad." A positive statement, "I'm doing better today," is more likely to evoke, "You're looking good," or "May I help?" or "Keep up the good work." These types of responses will do you more good. Sometimes, you will be inclined to lap up the misery and sympathy. Sometimes that may be what you need. But in the long run, positive comments help develop a positive attitude and are more beneficial.

Another way to help your attitude is to try not to take everything personally. If someone cuts in line in front of you, it is very unlikely to be a personal insult against you. More likely, they have kids waiting in the car or some other emergency that made them in a hurry. Perhaps they *are* just rude, but it certainly isn't intended personally. They would have cut in line in front of anyone. Similarly, if someone doesn't seem particularly interested in what you're saying about arthritis, don't always take it personally. They may have a problem of their own weighing on their mind and wouldn't be particularly interested in anything you might be saying at the time. It doesn't mean that they are not interested in you. Other people have problems, too.

Anyway, the best people to talk to about arthritis are other people with arthritis. That's not to say that others cannot help, but people with arthritis can empathize. People tend to relate better to people with the same interests and experiences. That's why support groups are important. Join one, or start one. Find someone who will share gripe time with you. The rules for this interchange are as follows: (1) The gripee (listener) must just listen, not condone or refute, and (2) the griper must not get carried away and must end the gripe time on a positive note. If you are allowed to complain uninterrupted and begin listening to yourself, you may find your complaints humorous. If not, force yourself to see the humor in a situation. Sometimes what seemed to be a tragic situation can be humorous in retrospect.

Finally, a positive attitude can be developed by taking good care of yourself. Do something positive for yourself every day. Write down what you intend to do for yourself physically, emotionally, and intellectually.

Taking care of yourself *physically* includes eating well, resting, exercising, and taking proper medication. It also includes pampering yourself with long baths, a new hairdo, or buying some new clothes. It's hard to dispute the old saying that when you look good, you feel good. Looking your best helps your self-image and your attitude.

Taking care of yourself *emotionally* often involves relationships with other people. To feel loved makes you feel happy, but sometimes you have to work to deserve it. Generally, love is reciprocated. Promise yourself a minimum daily hug requirement. Spend time and energy developing relationships that are important to you. That doesn't mean you shouldn't be cordial and friendly to everyone. How can you discover new meaningful relationships if you don't give new acquaintances a chance? The point is that you probably shouldn't pour out your soul to the mail carrier. It is not likely that he or she will reciprocate, and you will probably be hurt by the reaction. Save you pouring out for your spouse or close friends, because these people will reciprocate. Then, be ready and willing to listen to their souls pouring out.

Taking care of yourself *intellectually* means stimulating that mass of gray matter in your head. Don't let arthritis be the only thing on your mind. Keep those synapses firing in your brain. Take a course, read the paper, perhaps write a letter to the editor. Know what's going on outside of you. One thing is for sure, you'll react one way or another. You may laugh at an article, or be angered by a crime, or be puzzled by a problem. You are thinking. Intellectual stimulation is very important in feeling worthwhile. Challenges and achievements promote a healthy attitude. Below are some examples of what you can do for yourself, physically, emotionally, and intellectually, every day. There is an infinite number. Think of some activities of your own.

Physical	*Emotional*	*Intellectual*
Go to beauty parlor/barber	Greet spouse with a giant hug	Read the newspaper
Buy a new dress/shirt	Listen to the kids	Write a letter to the editor
Eat out	Give a massage	Read a book
Work on the yard	Call someone for gripe time	Call a friend and argue an issue
Exercise		
Build something		Do a crossword puzzle
Take a long hot bath	Write a letter	Draw plans to build something
Get a massage	Visit a sick friend	

You noticed that the activities in these three columns are not really separate at all and begin to overlap? Good, you're getting the idea.

Learn to Pick and Choose Your Stresses

Remember that some stress is important in order to achieve goals. But how do you choose what is worthwhile stress?

To decide whether you should feel stress or not, you must put things in perspective. What if you had only one month to live? What would you do differently? Asking yourself these questions can really help you distinguish what is and isn't important to you. Your list should include you as being very important. There are any number of things—family, friends, work, religion—that you consider worth fighting for. Remember, though, that you cannot fight everything. You must find a balance. Accept that some things are bigger than you; that some things are never done. You cannot alter the world, but you do make a difference.

Make another list of your talents and abilities. These may include talents in the fine arts (music, painting, etc.), a flair for politics, getting people to see your viewpoint, being a good organizer, the ability to help others, and thousands of other qualities that make you unique. After discovering these abilities, decide what you can realistically accomplish and go for it. If you have serious doubts that you can't do it, you probably can't. The important thing here, too, is balance. Don't expect too much from yourself, but don't expect too little either.

Once you have discovered what is important to you and have evaluated your abilities, you can decide whether you should feel stress or not. Anything that enhances these things, directly or indirectly, is probably worthwhile stress. Anything else is a waste of energy.

This requires some major evaluation of yourself, your goals, your dreams, and your relationships. But what about some of those outside interferences? You must learn when to say yes and when to say no. These are difficult decisions. Everyone has things they must do to please someone else, be it a boss, a spouse, a child, or a friend. You cannot be totally selfish and always do things only for yourself. You may sit through a Little League game, go to a dinner because of your job, or drive a friend somewhere. There are many such things that you really should do, and that's okay. If a situation is important to someone you care about, then indirectly it is important to you.

But there are things that are not really important to you or to anyone that you care about that you may feel pressured into doing. For instance, someone calls and asks you to go somewhere or do something. You know down to your bones that you do not want to do it and that your life will not change if you don't, but if you say "No," this person will be angry at you. If you say "Yes," you will be miserable and set yourself up for anxiety, frustration, and stress. How do you decide? Well, who is more important here? Look at it this way. If you do it, the person will eventually forget about it. If you don't do it, the person will eventually forget about it.

People who like you like you no matter what. People who don't like you, don't like you no matter what. There are people who will not like you even if you offer them your head on a platter. On the other hand, people who really like you will understand your refusal and still like you even when you are unlikeable sometimes. Those are the people deserving of your time and energy and the ones with whom you want to work on a relationship.

Anyway, there are enough situations that give you no choice. Don't force yourself to do things that you really don't have to do when you really don't want to do them.

After all this talk about stress, that's what it's really all about, isn't it? People feel stress when they don't get to do what they want to do. A stressful life is one in which one *never* gets to do what one wants. Realistically, no one gets to do what he or she wants all the time. But there's that balance again. If you *never* get what you want, you probably have a problem with stress. But how do you find a balance? You may need to start writing things down. Somehow, seeing things in black and white makes things easier to accomplish. Set goals for yourself daily, write them down, then accomplish them. A suggestion is to make columns of Have To, Should Do, and Want To. For example:

Have To	Should Do	Want To
Pay bills	Clean house	Nap
Take care of children	Laundry	Read a book
Go to work	Write letters	Go swimming

Absolutely everyone has Have To's every day. No big deal. Write them down, do them, and check them off when they are done. There will be a certain amount of satisfaction simply in the accomplishment of these tasks. A real problem lies in the Should Do column. There are always a million and one things in the Should Do column. No one can do a million and one things, but most of us try, and therefore we never get to the Want To column. Nothing in the Should Do column needs to be checked off on any given day. The Should Do column should simply be a list of options and reminders. When tasks in the Should Do column begin looming, move them over to the Have To column and do them. If the laundry sits in the Should Do column for five days, for goodness sake, put the laundry in the Have To column on the sixth day. On any given day, you will have the Have To's and the Want To's all checked. Be realistic in what you expect. Your Should

Do column will probably be the longest, and the other columns should not exceed what is humanly possible to accomplish in one day. There will be days when all you get done is the Have To's because there is simply so much to do. That's okay. Feel proud of yourself for all that you accomplished. There will be another day in which you get to do mostly Want To's. The important thing is that you get to do what you want on a regular basis.

This procedure seems simple, and maybe you already do it in your head. But try writing it down to actually see how much you get to do what you want. After all, it's pretty difficult to do what you want if you don't know what you want in the first place. By writing it down, you make your Want To's as important as your Have To's (and they are), and you are more apt to do them.

8 Rest and Exercise

ℵℵℵℵ

One of the benefits of exercise is that it makes you aware of your body. Boy, are you aware—Ugh. Those little aches and pains, though, are muscles making themselves known after being neglected for a long time. The initial shock wears off, and once those muscles have your attention they don't complain so much. In fact, if you really stick with it, you will find that you feel better when you exercise, and worse when you don't. If your muscles have been dormant for a long time, you will need to start slowly. It is a good idea to consult a physician before beginning your program, but generally if you start slowly and gradually build to a more strenuous routine, there shouldn't be a problem. It may seem ridiculous at first, only a few minutes, but remember it takes time to see results. Olympic decathlon participants do not begin training one week before the Olympics!

Recently there has been some concern over whether exercise can cause arthritis. With proper warm-up and stretching and the use of proper equipment (shoes, bicycles, etc.), there is no reason to believe that exercising will cause arthritis. What should cause some concern is repetitive injuries and improper treatment of injuries. Repetitive awkward motions, motions unnatural to joint movement, also may predispose a person to developing arthritis. An example of this is Little-Leaguer's elbow. Pitching can be a repetitive awkward motion, unnatural to the elbow's normal movement.

Does that mean that exercise for a person who already has arthritis may be detrimental? No, exercise is very beneficial in the treatment of arthritis. It strengthens the muscles supporting the joints and is important in maintaining full movement of joints, particularly those in danger of losing function. Again, proper warm-up and stretching and proper equipment are essential.

The key may be modification rather than elimination. For example, if tennis is your favorite sport, you need not give up the game. You may need to play more doubles than singles. You should take your medication the day of a match and for several days afterward. Even people with severe arthritis or who have artificial joints can participate in active exercise, such as walking, bicycling, golfing, swimming, and even cross-country skiing. People with a hip replacement, however, should avoid horseback riding because of the risk of dislocation.

Exercise is another facet of your responsibility for yourself. It is part of maintaining your body and feeling well. Exercise is not synonymous with fatigue. In fact, it can be quite exhilarating, which will help you develop a positive attitude about yourself and your body. There are many forms of exercise, but their benefits are cardiovascular fitness, strength, and flexibility. Cardiovascular exercise strengthens the heart by increasing the heart rate for a number of minutes and then gradually lowering it to normal. Aerobics is one type of cardiovascular exercise. A minimum of twenty minutes of aerobics, three times a week, is suggested for cardiovascular fitness. You may or may not be able to do aerobic exercises, depending on the severity of your arthritis. If you are able, by all means do it at your doctor's suggestion. But if you cannot do aerobic exercises, that does not let you off the hook. No one is really incapable of exercise because there are so many forms and varieties, and the amount depends on the individual.

Exercise involving strength and flexibility can be adapted to meet nearly anyone's needs. Exercise for strength does not necessarily mean body building. Simple, repetitive movement of a joint through its full range of motion will strengthen the muscles that support that particular joint. Flexibility exercises are stretching motions that can be particularly beneficial for arthritis sufferers who are besieged by stiffness. Stretching helps to limber you up as well as strengthen those muscles involved. Stretching exercises are simple and easy and accomplish two of the three benefits of exercise—flexibility and strength. Besides, stretching feels good. Everyone stretches. You may just need to modify your stretching to make it more beneficial. At this basic level, anyone can exercise.

Exercise can also improve your posture. Good posture can actually help your arthritis and be achieved by being aware of how you sit and stand, then correcting and practicing good posture. But exercise will also help improve your posture, even without your awareness.

Exercise is important for everyone, but the benefits for a person with arthritis are too great to delay starting a program for even another day.

Now that you know why exercise is so beneficial for you and your arthritis—for attitude, flexibility, posture, and strength—you really should feel guilty for not doing it. While you may not be happy about this new dose of guilt, guilt is an excellent motivator for accepting responsibility for yourself and your health.

Still not convinced? There is one more option that may persuade you to get out of the crowd of spectators and become a participant. A relatively new form of exercise that is growing in popularity is water exercise. Water exercise programs are popping up across the country, and have gained appeal since movement in water is less painful and generally more fun. You will enjoy the outing, meet people, and benefit from the exercise. Contact your local Arthritis Foundation chapter for the program nearest you.

All of this exercise stuff is fine and well, but you have arthritis and your joints are not always cooperative. You do have some special needs and concerns. You may need to do specific exercises for specific joints. Discuss this with your doctor. He or she can instruct you on what exercises to do for a specific joint and when to do them. Remember, if you can't do it yourself, seek help. Physical therapists are available at most hospitals. They will exercise a joint for you and show you or your family the proper procedures for specific joint exercises.

Because you have arthritis, you will also be more aware of the need for rest. During very active phases of your disease, you may not be able to exercise at all. Knowing when to rest is important and very often not a conscious decision at all. You are in severe pain and exercise is out of the question. However, utilizing rest periods to the maximum can help to relieve your discomfort. This involves learning *how* to rest a specific joint effectively. Your doctor can instruct you on some specifics, such as whether the joint should be elevated or not. But there are some simple things you can do to relieve the pain while you rest. Using hot and cold therapy is one method. Generally, heat achieves better results, but some people experience relief from the numbing effect of cold. Wet heat is often recommended over dry heat. Wet heat involves soaking towels in hot water and placing the heat pack on your joint. Wet heat also includes hot baths, which obviously soothes a greater number of joints than a hot pack. Dry heat therapy includes the use of electrical heating implements or heating pads. A couple of precautions are worth mentioning. First, be sure to place the heating pad on top of the particular joint. Do not lie on the device. Your body weight could produce a burn on your skin. Second, a person who has an artificial replacement or implant containing metal should not use heating pads. The metal inside the implant will conduct heat and could cause burns inside the joints.

Heat is generally more effective than cold, but if cold packs seem to relieve your pain, use the same procedure of soaking towels in cold water and placing them on the joint, or placing joints in cold water.

Obviously, any specific questions you have about hot and cold therapy can be best answered by your doctor.

Because you have arthritis, you may have concerns about whether the pain you feel when exercising is appropriate or not. Generally, mild pain experienced a couple of days after exercising is normal. The pain that should concern you is pain that you experience during the exercise or severe pain that persists for days.

Your body is the most reliable indicator of when you should exercise and when you should rest. If it feels good, do it. If it is painful, stop. If the pain persists, consult your physician.

Since you are relying on your body as an indicator, a very important question comes to mind. Will taking aspirin or NSAIDS mask any pain that would suggest discontinuing exercise? Generally, these agents are not potent enough to mask a pain that signals serious injury. If you are on other medication and are concerned about this, ask your doctor.

So you really should exercise, but when? When you exercise is entirely up to you, but do make it a part of your daily routine. Setting a specific time helps to make it a habit, and we all know how strong habits can be. We generally think of habits as something bad, but there are good habits as well. If you head for the coffee pot as soon as you stumble out of bed, that is a habit. You needn't break that habit, just create a new one. Perhaps you could exercise before coffee, making coffee your reward. Morning has many advantages as a set time for exercise. You probably have to go to work and won't have much opportunity during the day. By the time you get home, there's dinner, cleaning up, and you may be too tired. But the best reason for morning exercise is that you may awaken stiff and in pain. Getting out on the wrong side of the bed, so to speak, can set the mood for the whole day. Lie in bed for a while and stretch (always gently) every muscle in your body.

We recommend a series of exercises designed to help you get out on the right side of the bed. We suggest that you begin your program the minute your eyes are opened.

The following series of exercises are ones that almost anyone who has arthritis can and should do. The first series of exercises are done lying down. You move to a sitting position for the second series. They were designed to be done in bed, and getting out of bed, since this can be an important time for a person who has arthritis and awakens with morning stiffness. It is a good idea to do the series the first thing in the morning, and possibly in reverse order at night to relieve tension and relax. The series can be committed to memory after practice and does not necessarily have to be done in bed. The exercises can be done almost anywhere, at any time, with some modification. (However, do not drop to the floor in a crowded restaurant. It does tend to create a certain amount of hysteria.)

Some Pointers before You Begin

1. It is important to do these exercises in a slow, flowing movement, stopping when you feel a stretch. Never bounce a stretch. This will cause the joint to move farther than necessary. The goal is to move the joint through its full range of mo-

tion, to strengthen the muscles surrounding the joint, and achieve flexibility.

2. Be aware of your posture when doing the sitting exercises; keep your back straight and your feet flat on the floor.

3. Incorporate some breathing and visualization skills into your exercises. Some of the illustrations include drawings of joints to help you imagine what is going on inside of your skin. Visualize the specific body part that you are exercising; inhale as you tighten muscles and exhale when you relax.

4. Concentrate on what you are doing—don't rush it. Think about the good things you are doing for your joints and your body. Give yourself time to wake up, and then get out on the right side of the bed.

Obviously, these series of exercises will not be enough for most of you. There are books, television shows, literally hundreds of sources for more strenuous exercise. Develop a routine that fits your needs and make up a third series to be completed after these two sets. The series suggested here should help get you started on an exercise program. The rest depends on your motivation and abilities.

Series One

1. Stretch
Arms high above head—Reach—Bring toes back toward body—Hold 10 seconds—Relax—Repeat.

2. Angels in the Snow
Swing arms to shoulder height while opening legs far apart—Put legs back together and hands at sides—Repeat 5 times. You must be careful with this exercise—if your spouse still happens to be in bed.

136

3. Pelvic Tilt

Bend knees—Push lower back flat to floor (or bed)—
Relax—Repeat 5 times.

4. Knee to Chest

Bring right knee to chest—Hold onto thigh—Lower
leg—Repeat 5 times. Repeat procedure with left leg.

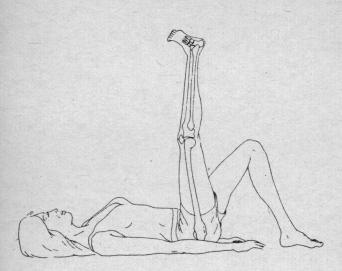

5. Straight-Leg Raise

Slowly raise right leg toward ceiling (keep left leg bent)—Point toes toward ceiling, then toward body 3 times—Slowly lower leg, then lift again—Do ankle circles, clockwise and counter-clockwise. Repeat procedure with left leg.

6. Curl-up

*Put hands on thigh—Lift chest and slide hands up
to knees—Return to floor (bed)—Relax—Repeat 2
more times.*

7. Twists

*Put arms out in a T, knees bent and together—
Gently roll to right side—Bring knees back to center
and roll to left side—Repeat 2 more times. Be sure
to keep shoulders flat on floor (bed).*

Series Two

1. Puppet
Swing arms above head.

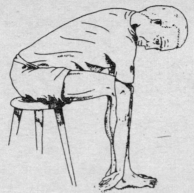

2. Puppet II
*Swing arms and bend at waist—Let head drop—
Relax as puppet.*

3. Puppet III
*Sit up and swing arms out to side—Bring hands
back to center—Repeat 3 times.*

4. Shoulder Shrugs
Bring shoulders up toward ears—Lower and relax—Repeat 5 times.

5. Head Semi-Circles
Start with chin on right shoulder—Swing down along chest to left shoulder, then back to right—Do 10 times.

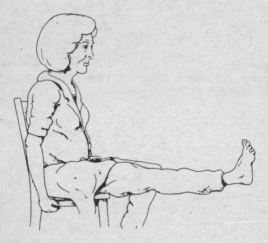

6. Leg Lifts
Lift right leg—Bring toe toward body—Return to floor. Lift left leg—Bring toe toward body—Return to floor. Alternate, doing each leg 5 times.

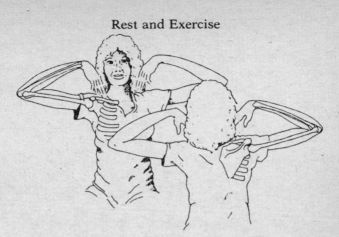

7. Elbow Circles

Place hands on shoulders, elbows shoulder height—
Do 5 circles forward—5 circles backward.

8. Side Bend

Hands on shoulder—Lean
toward right hip—Return to
center—Lean toward left
hip—Repeat 5 times.

9. Sitting Twist
*Keep back straight—Turn trunk to right and swing
arms up and out—Head follows arms—Return to
center—Put hands in lap—Turn trunk to left and
swing arms up and out—Head follows arms—
Return to center—Repeat 5 times.*

10.
End exercise session with 5 more puppets.

Some Suggestions

1. Pick a specific time to exercise to form a habit. Morning is recommended. Taking a hot shower or bath following exercise can also help limber up stiff joints and muscles.
2. Use stretching exercises along with your relaxation and visualization skills frequently throughout the day to reduce tension. Give yourself little breaks.
3. Use exercises as a diversion to stop thinking about food, problems, and your arthritis—to help break a pattern of complaining.
4. Don't exercise when you need to rest and vice versa. Let your body be your guide. Always seek professional help if a severe pain persists.
5. Don't be too hard on yourself if you slack off sometimes—just keep trying.

9 Diet and Nutrition

Topics in Basic Nutrition
Fat and Cholesterol
Sugar
Calories
Fiber
Salt
Vitamins and Minerals
Thirst Quenchers
Water
Caffeine Drinks
Alcohol
Artificially Sweetened Beverages

Eating-Well Calendar

Menus
Breakfast Breakthrough
Munch-a-Lunch
Super Suppers

Recipes
Breakfast Recipes
Lunch Recipes
Supper Recipes

Pantry Particulars

Some Suggestions

⧉⧉⧉⧉

Of all unproven remedies for arthritis, those of diet and nutrition are the most recognized and widespread. The lists of new diets—nutritional and mineral supplements to cure or prevent arthritis—grow almost daily. The fact is that arthritis is an illness whose cause and cure are unknown. Therefore, unproven ideas can be very attractive.

Though many diets have been scientifically tested, there is no proof at this time that the addition or deletion of any vitamins and minerals will prevent or cure arthritis. While it is a good idea to take vitamins, megadoses of some vitamins are potentially dangerous. Excessive amounts of certain vitamins, such as A and D, are not easily expelled from the body. Fortunately, the body is capable of ridding itself of excess vitamins in most cases.

Food allergies have also been suggested as an explanation for arthritis. Elimination diets have been tried and have not proven to be helpful with most arthritis. Diet is important in gout, which can be aggravated by foods high in purine content, such as kidney, liver, sweet breads, and sardines. People with gout should avoid these foods as well as avoid excessive amounts of alcohol, which may precipitate an acute attack.

A special diet may also help an overweight person with arthritis. In arthritis that involves the weight-bearing joints—spine, hips, knees—excessive body weight can increase wear on the joints and cause more pain. People who are overweight are most likely to suffer from osteoarthritis. A diet can be adjusted under a doctor's supervision, and weight reduction can indirectly help the arthritis. A person who is overweight and also has arthritis is prey to two kinds of quackery. Along with diets claiming to cure arthritis, the person will be deluged by plans that claim to be able to reduce weight overnight. If you have arthritis and need to lose weight, you should consult a physician to establish the best personal diet for you. Because of your special needs, an over-the-counter diet may not be appropriate.

An effective diet for arthritis is basically a healthy diet for anyone. A well-balanced diet that includes proper calorie intake is the best diet. Like anyone else, you should maintain ideal body weight. A multivitamin can be taken to fulfill the daily requirements of most vitamins.

While what you eat (or don't eat) will not cure arthritis, your diet is one of the ways to be responsible for yourself and gain control over your health and, indirectly, your arthritis. We all eat—we have to—but what we eat is a choice. You have before you a vegetable platter and a chocolate cake. It is your choice whether to eat the vegetables, the cake, or to eat it all. Almost everyone knows what should be done, but *nobody* does what he or she is supposed to do all the time. The important thing, once again, is the long haul. If you always eat it all, you will have a weight problem. If you always eat the cake, you will have a nutritional problem. But if you always eat the vegetables when in fact you want the cake, you are setting yourself up for frustration. After all, chocolate cake is one of life's little pleasures. As long as you maintain a balance, you can splurge sometimes. Eating well helps to make a person healthy, and you are a person first. Good nutrition helps you and therefore helps your arthritis.

Topics in Basic Nutrition

To achieve good nutrition, you must first know what good nutrition means. Basically, nutrition is what you eat and drink every day and how the nutrients in that food are used by the body. The human body works better and lasts longer when it is provided with the 50 nutrients it needs every day. These nutrients are divided into six groups:

carbohydrates protein
fat vitamins
minerals water

The difference between good nutrition and poor nutrition depends on your choice of foods.

Most of us have established our eating habits based on taste sensations we *learned* to enjoy. As a result, our diets have become high in fat, salt, and sugar and low in vitamins, minerals, and fiber. Fortunately, you have control over your food choices and can *learn* to enjoy foods with less fat, sugar, and salt by modifying your nutritional life-style. Good nutrition means giving your body all the nutrients it needs, in the right amounts, when it needs them. This is achieved by your food choices—your diet. It is hard to apply basic nutrition principles unless you know where you are going wrong and how to modify your food choices to achieve a healthy diet. Summarized, the following are the major areas in the American diet where change is needed.

Fat and Cholesterol

Americans presently consume about 42% of their calories from fat and eat more than 500 milligrams of cholesterol each day. Diets high in fat and cholesterol have been associated with high blood cholesterol and triglycerides (fat), thus increasing the risk of heart disease. The American Heart Association recommends that the general public reduce fat intake to less than 30% of total calories and cholesterol to less than 300 milligrams per day.

Sugar

Sugar is the simplest form of carbohydrate and composes about 25% of our daily calories. The major health hazard from eating too much sugar is tooth decay. Empty calorie foods such as sweets and desserts can contribute to extra pounds and result in being overweight. Limiting sugar intake to 10% of daily calories is a healthy goal.

Calories

Individual calorie needs vary according to age, frame size, sex, and daily activity. When more calories are consumed than the body needs, weight is gained. Obesity is associated with high blood pressure, increased levels of blood fat (triglycerides) and cholesterol, increased risks of heart disease, and stroke. For persons with arthritis, increased weight causes undue stress on joints that may already be painful. A gradual weight loss of one to two pounds per week is healthy and more likely to be permanent. This is best accomplished through a reduction in calories and an increase in exercise.

Fiber

The average American diet is low in fiber. Low fiber intake has been associated with chronic constipation and diverticulosis and possibly increases the risk of developing cancer of the colon. Eating seven to eight high fiber foods daily is a realistic goal. Consumption of complex carbohydrates such as dried beans, split peas, legumes, nuts, seeds, fruits, vegetables, whole grain breads, cereals, and bran will increase dietary fiber. The bulk provided by fiber increases meal satisfaction without the calories.

A word of caution.

1. Increase fiber intake gradually.
2. Drink six to eight glasses of water daily. Fiber and fluids work hand in hand.

Salt

The average American consumes too much sodium in the form of salt and processed foods. Excess sodium intake has been linked to high blood pressure. Some medicines prescribed for arthritis may cause fluid retention. A diet low in sodium can help prevent this.

Vitamins and Minerals

The interaction of vitamins and minerals helps regulate body processes. Loading up on one vitamin or mineral may interfere with this regulatory function. Fat soluble vitamins (vitamin A, D, E, and K) are stored in the body. An excess could result in harmful toxic levels. Excess water soluble vitamins (C and B complex vitamins) are eliminated from the body in urine, but recent evidence indicates that an excess of these vitamins may also have harmful side effects. The right proportion of all the *"natural"* vitamins and minerals needed for biochemical processes that take place in the body can be obtained from a well-balanced diet. If supplementing the diet is necessary, a vitamin-mineral supplement that provides 100% of the RDA for each nutrient listed is recommended.

Thirst Quenchers

Water

Sixty percent of our body weight comes from water. It creates the environment in which all of the body's chemical processes take place. Water provides the necessary fluid to keep joints mobile and is necessary to eliminate the waste products of digestion. Concentrate on drinking more than six glasses of clear water daily in addition to other fluids.

Caffeine Drinks

It is not uncommon for persons to consume more than 1000 milligrams of caffeine (seven or more cups of coffee) daily. Caffeine is a drug that stimulates the nervous system. Jitters, upset stomach, insomnia, and elevated blood sugar are some of the consequences of a high caffeine intake. Anti-inflammatory medication can be irritating to the stomach, and caffeine will only compound the problem. Try to limit caffeine consumption to less than 250 milligrams per day. The chart below lists the caffeine content of some common beverages.

Beverage	Milligrams of Caffeine per Serving
Coffee, drip	150 mg / 5 oz.
Coffee, instant	60 mg / 5 oz.
Coffee, decaffeinated	3 mg / 5 oz.
Tea, black, 5 min. brew	46 mg / 5 oz.
Tea, black, 1 min. brew	28 mg / 5 oz.
Tea, instant	50 mg / 8 oz.
Cocoa	20 mg / 8 oz.

Carbonated Beverages	
Coca-cola	55 mg / 12 oz.
Mountain Dew	55 mg / 12 oz.
Dr. Pepper	52 mg / 12 oz.
Tab	48 mg / 12 oz.
Pepsi-cola	41 mg / 12 oz.
Diet Pepsi	36 mg / 12 oz.
RC–100	0 mg / 12 oz.
Diet 7-up	0 mg / 12 oz.

Alcohol

Alcoholic beverages tend to be high in calories and low in nutrients. Heavy drinking may have serious consequences such as cirrhosis of the liver, obesity, malnutrition, and social problems. One or two drinks daily does not appear to cause harm in adults. If you drink, you should do so in moderation.

Artificially Sweetened Beverages

The most common artificial sweeteners used in beverages are aspartame (Nutrasweet) and saccharin. The Food and Drug Administration has approved the use of both substances in beverages and other food products.

Aspartame   This is a sweetener made from a combination of two amino acids, phenylalanine and aspartic acid. Aspartame is 180 times sweeter than sugar and does not leave a bitter aftertaste. Aspartame, however, is unstable at high temperatures and so cannot be used in baking products. Aspartame can be harmful to people with an inherited metabolic abnormality called phenylketonuria.

Saccharin   This is made from petroleum products and is 300 times sweeter than sugar. Saccharin also breaks down at high temperatures and has a bitter metallic aftertaste. Some research studies have shown a possible link between saccharin use and bladder cancer.

If an artificial sweetener is used, moderation is recommended. Two to three servings daily of food or drink containing either of these substances is probably safe for most people. Drinking a six-pack of diet soda and using four to five packages of dry sweetener every day is *not* moderation. Here are some suggestions and recipes for healthy, nutritious, thirst-quenching beverages.

—Try a tall glass of ice water served with a twist of lemon or lime.

—Simple but nutritious fruit and vegetable juices.

—Mix club soda or diet 7-up with your favorite juice, such as grape, apple, cranberry, or pineapple. Garnish with mint leaves or a slice of orange, lemon, or lime. Serve in a frosty glass.

—Fruit juice combos can be appealing. For a hot beverage, heat pineapple and grapefruit juices with stick cinnamon and cloves.

—Spice up your steamy cup of decaffeinated coffee or tea with cinnamon and cloves.

—Try this Hot Spicy Cider:

2 cups water
2 cups unsweetened apple juice
1 cup unsweetened orange juice
4 sticks cinnamon
1 tsp whole cloves
1 tsp whole allspice

Combine water and juices in a large saucepan. Add spices tied loosely in a porous cloth. Cover and simmer 20 minutes. Remove the spices. Serve hot with a twist of orange peel.

Eating-Well Calendar

Eating well can mean eating yourself "well." Now that you know some of the things that may be wrong about your eating habits, you can take steps to correct them.

But your eating habits have been established over a period of years and changing those habits will not be easy or quick.

Following is an "Eating-Well Calendar" for the next year. Concentrate on a different area each month. The changes will not seem so overwhelming, and gradually you can achieve your ultimate goal of eating well.

Month	Nutritional Component to Change	Suggestions for Change
First	Fat	Limit beef, pork, poultry, and fish to a total of 6 oz daily. Increase use of fish and chicken in meals. Use lean cuts of meat.
Second	Sugar	*Cut* portion size of sugar, jelly, desserts, soda pop, jello, and candy *in half*. Eat them *half* as often.
Third	Salt	Do not use salt at the table. Try an herb shaker blend.
Fourth	Fiber	Eat a bran cereal for breakfast. Switch to whole-wheat bread.

Month	Nutritional Component to Change	Suggestions for Change
		Include more fresh vegetables.
Fifth	Caffeine	Switch to decaffeinated coffee, tea, and soda pop. Try drinking more water every day.
Sixth	Fat	Switch to low-fat milk products (skim milk, low-fat cheeses, plain yogurt). Limit egg yolks to 3 per week. Substitute 2 egg whites for one egg yolk. Use cholesterol-free egg substitutes in cooking.
Seventh	Sugar	Limit sweets to 10% of your calories. Example: 10% of 1500 calories = 150 calories 150 cals = 12 oz Pepsi or 1 small piece of cake or ½ cup ice cream or 2 medium cookies

Month	Nutritional Component to Change	Suggestions for Change
Eighth	Salt	Decrease consumption of salty foods (ham, bacon, sausage, lunch meats, hot dogs, salty snack crackers and peanuts, canned soups and bouillion, seasoned salts, soy sauce, catsup, and mustard).
Ninth	Fiber	Eat 2 fresh vegetables each day. Eat 3 fresh fruits daily. Try to include a daily serving of dried beans or legumes.
Tenth	Fat	Reduce added fat at the table and in recipes by ⅓ to ½ (margarine, mayonnaise, salad dressing). Limit fried foods to 2–3 times per week.
Eleventh	Salt	Reduce salt in cooking by one half. ½ tsp rather than 1 tsp. 4 shakes rather than 8 shakes.

Month	Nutritional Component to Change	Suggestions for Change
Twelfth	Alcohol	If you drink, limit to one or two drinks per day.

Summary

1. Eat a variety.
2. Keep your portion size moderate.

Menus

You have a pretty good idea about good nutrition and how to achieve it, but these general guidelines may not be enough to get you by day to day. Following are some specific menus for 14 days. Obviously, these menus are not intended to be repeated over and over through the course of a year. They are, however, suggestions to get you started. Once you get the hang of it, your imagination can kick in and create an infinite number of menus that are good for you.

The following menus are low in fat, cholesterol, salt, and sugar. Any breakfast, lunch, and supper combination will provide approximately 1200 to 1350 calories and all the nutrients needed for a healthier you. If your caloric intake need exceeds this level, portion sizes may be increased or nutritious snacks may be included. Milk or milk products are included in each menu to meet calcium needs. If you do not use milk products, consult your physician about calcium supplementation.

Breakfast Breakthrough

Eat well by starting each day with a good breakfast. You will work better, have more energy, and be less tempted by high calorie snacks at mid-morning. Recipes for all starred (*) items follow the menu ideas.

1. *2 Whole-Wheat Pancakes
   *½ cup Strawberry Sauce
   1 cup skim milk

2. 1 cup cooked oatmeal
   2 Tbsp raisins
   1 tsp margarine
   1 cup skim milk

3. 2 toasted wheat bagel halves
   1½ Tbsp Neufchatel cream cheese
   1 apple, sliced
   1 cup skim milk

4. ½ cup bran flakes
   ½ banana, sliced
   1 slice whole-wheat toast
   1 tsp margarine
   1 cup skim milk

5. 2 wheat English muffin halves, toasted
   2 tsp peanut butter
   ½ banana
   1 pkg sugar-free cocoa

6. 2 slices whole-wheat toast
    2 Tbsp plain low-fat yogurt with ¼ tsp cin-
        namon and ½ pkg Equal spread on top
        of warm toast
    ¼ cantaloupe (or fresh fruit in season)
    1 cup skim milk

Menus 1 through 6 will meet the diabetic food exchanges for 1 skim milk, 1 fruit, 2 bread, and 1 fat,
or approximately 300 calories.

7. *2 slices of Banana French Toast
    ½ cup plain low-fat yogurt flavored with ½
        tsp vanilla and ½ pkg Equal
    1 pkg sugar-free cocoa

8. *2 Whole-Wheat Pancakes wrapped around
    *2½ oz Fresh Breakfast Sausage links (may
        be warmed in microwave oven)
    1 fresh orange
    1 cup skim milk

Menus 7 and 8 meet the diabetic food exchanges
for 1 skim milk, 1 fruit, 2 bread, 1 oz meat, and 1 fat,
or approximately 370 calories.

9. ½ wheat English muffin, toasted and
        topped with:
        1 egg fried in 1 tsp margarine
        1 oz low-fat processed American cheese
    ½ cup orange juice

10. ½ wheat English muffin, toasted
    2 Tbsp peanut butter

½ cup orange juice
1 cup skim milk

11. *1 Bran Muffin
*1 oz Fresh Breakfast Sausage patty
¼ cantaloupe (or fresh fruit in season)
1 cup skim milk

12. *¼" slice Lemon Yogurt Bread
1 hard-cooked egg
1½ cups peach yogurt (blend 1 cup plain
low-fat yogurt with ½ cup juice-packed
peaches, 1 pkg Equal and vanilla extract
to taste)

13. *½ cup leftover casserole (see lunch and
supper menus and recipes) or
*1 Mini-Pizza
½ grapefruit
1 cup skim milk

14. *1 Bran Muffin
1 poached egg
1 sliced pear
1 cup skim milk

Menus 9 through 14 meet the diabetic food exchanges for 1 skim milk, 1 fruit, 1 bread, 1 oz meat,
and 1 fat, or approximately 300 calories.

Munch-a-Lunch

Eating a small but balanced lunch will calm hunger
pangs and give you energy in the afternoon. Here is
a variety of hot and cold menus, some brown-bagable
and all easy to prepare. Enjoy each bite!

Diet and Nutrition

1. 1 stuffed tomato:
    (½ cup 2% low-fat cottage cheese with 1
    Tbsp grated carrot, chopped green pep-
    per, or chives)
    *½ cup "Rooney Tooney" Salad
    1 cup skim milk
    12 fresh grapes

2. 1 tuna a la mode platter (*½ cup Tuna
    Salad in ¼ cantaloupe)
    4 whole-grain crackers
    ½ cup lemon low-fat yogurt (use plain yo-
    gurt, lemon extract, and Equal)
    *½ cup Marinated Bean Salad
    ½ cup skim milk

3. *¾ cup Baked Lentils with Cheese
    celery sticks
    ½ cup citrus fruit salad (orange and grape-
    fruit sections)

4. 1 mini whole-wheat turkey-veggie pita
    (with 2 oz sliced turkey, alfalfa sprouts,
    grated or chopped vegetables)
    *½ cup Carrot Raisin Salad
    1 cup skim milk

5. *1 cup Yummy Chili
    2 slices juice-packed pineapple
    1 cup skim milk

6. *1 Baked Potato Pizazz
    ½ cup broccoli spears
    1 fresh pear
    1 cup skim milk

7. Unique Chef Salad with:
   1 oz low-fat cheese
   ¼ cup flaked tuna or cooked cubed chicken
   ¼ cup garbanzo beans
   1 Tbsp sunflower seeds
   2 Tbsp raisins
   3 Tbsp Kraft Zesty Italian Reduced-Calorie Dressing
   1 cup skim milk

8. *Broccoli Mushroom Strata
   *1 cup Fruity Tufu Salad

9. *1¼ cups Barley Beef Soup
   1½ cups Peach Yogurt (blend 1 cup plain low-fat yogurt, ½ cup juice-packed peaches, 1 pkg Equal, and 1 tsp vanilla)

10. *1 Turkey Sausage Pita
    1 fresh pear
    1 cup skim milk

Lunch menus 1 through 10 meet the diabetic food exchanges for 1 skim milk, 1 fruit, 1 vegetable, 1 bread, 2 oz meat, and 1 fat, or approximately 400 calories.

11. *1 Garden Chicken and Cheese Sandwich
    1 fresh apple
    1 cup skim milk

12. *1 Bulgur Salad Pita
    Peanut butter celery sticks (2 Tbsp peanut butter spread in celery sticks)
    ¼ cantaloupe (or fresh fruit in season)
    1 cup skim milk

13. Meat loaf sandwich with:
      2 oz leftover Meat Loaf (see supper reci-
      pes)
      2 slices whole-wheat bread
      1 Tbsp low-salt spaghetti sauce
   carrot sticks
   fresh fruit in season
   1 cup skim milk

14. *1 cup Macaroni and Cheese
    *½ cup Kidney Bean Salad
     ½ cup cinnamon applesauce (mix unsweet-
     ened applesauce with ground cinnamon)

Lunch menus 11 through 14 meet the diabetic food
exchanges for 1 skim milk, 1 fruit, 1 vegetable, 2 bread,
2 oz meat, and 1 fat, or approximately 470 calories.

Super Suppers

End the day with a nutrition-packed taste sensation,
but be sure to control portion sizes. Healthy foods have
calories, too.

1. *2 Beef Tacos
    carrot sticks
    ½ cup juice-packed fruit cocktail

2. *Pineapple Chicken Stir Fry
    ½ cup brown rice
    ½ wheat bagel, toasted
    1 Tbsp Neufchatel cream cheese
    10 bing cherries
    1 cup skim milk

3. *Spinach Rice Quiche
    1 cup tomato juice
    *1 Bran Muffin
    1 tsp margarine
    *Strawberry Tapioca Parfait

4. *2 oz Pan Fried Fish
    1 baked potato with 1 tsp margarine and 1
       Tbsp yogurt
    ½ cup green peas and fresh mushrooms
    ½ cup fresh sliced peaches or fresh fruit in
       season
    1 cup skim milk

5. 2 mini-pizzas made with:
    2 whole-wheat English muffin halves
    ¼ cup low-salt pizza sauce
    ⅓ cup browned sausage (see breakfast rec-
       ipes)
    ¼ cup grated mozzarella cheese
    ¼ cup chopped green pepper (optional)
    ½ cup green beans
    ½ cup orange sections

6. 2 oz baked pork chop
    ½ cup rice pilaf
    ¼ cup mixed vegetables
    *½ cup Creamy Coleslaw
    *1 Bran Muffin (see breakfast recipes)
    1 tsp margarine
    1 large fresh plum
    1 cup skim milk

7. *2 oz Crispy Oven-Baked Chicken
    ½ cup stewed tomatoes
    2″ square of corn bread

       1 tsp margarine
    *1 serving of Apple Crisp

8. *1 serving of Zesty Spinach Lasagna
      tossed salad
      1 Tbsp diet salad dressing
    *1 Bran Muffin (see breakfast recipes)
    *1 Baked Apple
      1 cup skim milk

9. *2 oz Lemon-Herb Broiled Chicken
    *½ cup Bulgur Pilaf
     ⅓ cup corn
     1 sliced tomato salad
     1 cup skim milk

10. *2 oz Scandinavian Baked Fish
     ½ cup broccoli spears
      ½ cup corkscrew noodles with
      1 tsp margarine
      1 Tbsp Parmesan cheese
    *¼" slice Lemon Yogurt Bread (see break-
      fast recipes)
     fresh fruit in season
     1 cup skim milk

11. *Curried Chicken over:
      ½ cup brown rice
     ½ cup carrot coins
     diet lime-pear gelatin salad (use diet lime
      gelatin and unsweetened canned pears)
     1 cup skim milk
    *1 Healthy Cookie

12. *1 serving Favorite Meat Loaf
     ⅓ cup yams seasoned with cinnamon and
      1 tsp margarine

    1 cup cauliflower-broccoli medley (½ cup
       each cauliflower and broccoli flowerets)
    1 oz angel food cake with ½ cup fresh or
       frozen unsweetened strawberries
    1 cup skim milk

13. *1 cup Tabouli, Bean, and Cheese Casserole
    spinach salad with lemon juice
    1 fresh orange
    1 cup skim milk

14. *Turkey Meatball Sandwich
    ½ cup beets
    tossed salad with 1 Tbsp diet dressing
  *½ cup Pumpkin Custard

All supper menus meet the diabetic food exchanges for 1 skim milk, 1 fruit, 2 vegetables, 2 bread, 2 oz meat, and 1 fat, or approximately 500 calories.

Recipes

Breakfast Recipes

Whole-Wheat Pancakes

1⅓ cups whole-wheat flour	1⅓ cups skim milk
¾ tsp baking soda	1 Tbsp vinegar
¼ tsp salt (optional)	1 egg, beaten
	3 Tbsp oil

Add vinegar to milk. Let sit 1 minute. Add baking soda. Stir flour and salt together. Add milk to dry ingredients and mix well. Stir in egg and oil. Bake on hot griddle using ¼ cup batter per pancake. Makes 12 4″ pancakes. Store leftover cooked pancakes in freezer by layering pancakes with waxed paper. Wrap whole package in tinfoil or freezer paper.

Strawberry Sauce

8 oz unsweetened
  strawberries,
  fresh or frozen
½ cup orange juice

2 Tbsp cornstarch
Equal packets to
  taste

Thaw strawberries. Dissolve cornstarch in orange juice. Mix with strawberries. Cook on low heat or in microwave till thickened. Add Equal to desired sweetness.

Banana French Toast

1 egg, beaten
½ banana

cinnamon to taste
2 slices whole-wheat
  bread

Mash bananas. Mix with cinnamon. Combine egg with banana mixture. Dip bread into mixture and fry on both sides over low heat in nonstick pan. Top with yogurt.

Bran Muffins

1½ cups
  unprocessed bran
1 cup whole-wheat
  flour
1 tsp baking soda
2 tsp baking powder

1 egg, beaten
2 Tbsp oil
½ cup molasses
¾ cup skim milk
1 Tbsp vinegar

Add vinegar to milk; let set 5 minutes to sour. Mix dry ingredients. Mix egg, oil, molasses, and soured milk. Add milk mixture to dry ingredients. Blend just until moistened. Spoon into muffin tins, filling ⅔ full. Bake in 400° oven for 15 minutes. Yields 12 muffins. Store leftovers in freezer.

Fresh Breakfast Sausage

1½ lbs fresh ground
  turkey
¼ cup parsley
1 tsp sage
1 tsp paprika
¼ tsp salt (optional)

½ tsp onion powder
½ tsp thyme
½ tsp fennel seed
½ tsp pepper

In medium bowl, combine all ingredients. Shape ½ lb into 4 1-oz patties to be used in breakfast menu #11. Shape ½ lb into 8 ½-oz links to be used in breakfast menu #8. Remaining 1 lb may be used for Mini-Pizzas in supper menu #5 and for Turkey Sausage Pita in lunch menu #10. In 12″ skillet over medium heat, cook patties till they are browned on both sides and cooked throughout. Any uncooked sausage may be stored in refrigerator up to 2 days or store in freezer till ready to cook and use. Any leftover cooked sausage may also be stored in freezer.

Lemon Yogurt Bread

1½ cups white flour
1½ cups whole-
    wheat flour
½ tsp salt (optional)
1 tsp baking powder
3 eggs
¾ cup oil
¾ cup sugar

1 cup plain yogurt
1 cup lemon yogurt
2 Tbsp skim milk
1 Tbsp lemon
    extract
1 cup very finely
    chopped almonds
    (optional)

Sift together white flour, salt, and baking powder. Stir in whole-wheat flour and nuts; set aside. Beat eggs in a large bowl; add oil and sugar; beat well. Add yogurts, milk, and extract. Spoon into two well-greased loaf pans, or one large well-greased Bundt pan. Bake in preheated oven at 325° for 1 hour. Freezes well.

Lunch Recipes

"Rooney Tooney" Salad

2 cups cooked whole-
wheat corkscrew
pasta
¼ cup broccoli
flowerets

¼ cup sliced
mushrooms
¼ cup sliced carrots

Marinade:
¼ cup vinegar
1½ tsp prepared
Dijon-style
mustard
¼ tsp celery seed
⅛ tsp garlic powder

1½ tsp parsley
⅛ tsp pepper
⅛ tsp salt (optional)
1 Tbsp Parmesan
cheese

Combine ingredients for marinade and mix well. Combine marinade with raw vegetables. Toss with cooked
cooled pasta. Refrigerate 1 hour to let flavors blend.

Tuna Salad

7 oz can water-packed tuna
2 Tbsp reduced-calorie mayonnaise-type salad dressing
1 Tbsp prepared Dijon-style mustard
¼ cup chopped celery
⅛ tsp black pepper
dash of Tabasco sauce (optional)
1 hard-cooked egg, diced

Combine all ingredients except egg; mix well. Gently stir in egg. Makes 4 servings.

Yummy Chili

½ lb ground beef
4 green onions, chopped
½ cup chopped green pepper
1 can (28 oz) whole tomatoes
1 can (6 oz) tomato paste
1 can (15 oz) chili-style beans
1 cup fresh mushrooms, sliced
2 tsp chili powder
⅛ tsp garlic powder
black pepper to taste

Brown ground beef with green onion and green pepper. Drain well. Add tomatoes, tomato paste, chili beans, mushrooms, and spices. Simmer on low for 30 to 60

minutes depending on how thick you like the chili.
Makes 4 servings.

Baked Lentils with Cheese

12 oz lentils, rinsed
2 cups water
1 bay leaf
1 tsp salt (optional)
¼ tsp pepper
⅛ tsp marjoram
⅛ tsp sage
⅛ tsp thyme
2 large onions,
    chopped
2 cloves garlic,
    minced
1 1-lb can tomatoes
2 large carrots,
    sliced ⅛" thick

½ cup thinly-sliced
    celery
1 green pepper,
    chopped
2 Tbsp finely
    chopped parsley
12 oz low-fat
    cheddar-type
    cheese, cubed (try
    Fisher Country
    Charm or Weight
    Watcher's
    Natural)

In a shallow baking dish, mix the lentils, water, bay
leaf, salt, pepper, marjoram, sage, thyme, onions, garlic,
and tomatoes. Then cover tightly with foil and bake
in a 375° oven for 30 minutes. Uncover, stir in carrots
and celery. Bake covered for 40 minutes or until vegetables are tender. Stir in green pepper and parsley.
Sprinkle cheese on top; bake uncovered for 5 minutes
or until cheese melts. Yields 6 servings.

Carrot Raisin Salad

3 cups grated
   carrots
½ cup raisins

⅓ cup reduced-
   calorie
   mayonnaise-type
   salad dressing
¼ tsp cinnamon

Mix grated carrots and raisins in a medium bowl. In a small bowl thoroughly mix salad dressing and cinnamon. Stir dressing mixture into carrots and raisins. Let marinate at least 2 hours in refrigerator before serving. Yields 6 ½-cup servings.

Marinated Bean Salad

1 can (1 lb) cut
   green beans
1 can (1 lb) cut wax
   beans
½ cup cider vinegar
2 packets Equal
1 tsp pickling spices

1 cup thinly sliced
   celery
1 small onion,
   chopped
2 Tbsp chopped
   green pepper
2 Tbsp chopped
   pimiento

Drain beans; reserve ½ cup liquid. In large bowl, combine reserved liquid, vinegar, Equal, and pickling spices. Add beans and remaining ingredients. Mix well.

Cover. Chill overnight, stirring occasionally. Makes 6 ½-cup servings.

Baked Potato Pizazz

1 small baked potato
2 oz grated farmer
cheese

¼ tsp thyme
¼ tsp dried or
chopped fresh dill
to taste

Halve baked potato and scoop out insides. Mix insides with cheese and seasonings, put back into skins. (Eat skins and all!)

Broccoli-Mushroom Strata

2 cups sliced fresh
mushrooms
2 cups chopped
broccoli
6 slices whole-wheat
bread, toasted
and cut into
quarters
4 slices low-fat
Swiss-flavored
processed cheese
4 slices low-fat
American
processed cheese

¼ cup chopped
pimiento, drained
2 Tbsp finely
chopped onion
1 cup egg substitute
2 cups skim milk
3 Tbsp all-purpose
flour
½ tsp dried basil,
crushed
¼ cup slivered
almonds, toasted
paprika

Cook broccoli and mushrooms in minimum amount of water. Drain well. Arrange half of the toasted bread quarters in the bottom of a 9 × 9 × 2 inch baking pan. Top with low-fat processed Swiss cheese, then broccoli and mushroom mixture. Layer low-fat processed American cheese, then sprinkle with pimiento and onion. Top with remaining bread quarters. In a bowl, lightly beat the egg substitute; stir in milk, flour, and basil. Pour over toasted bread and vegetables in the baking pan. Cover and chill at least 1 hour or overnight. Sprinkle toasted almonds over chilled mixture. Sprinkle lightly with paprika for color. Bake uncovered in 325° oven about 50 minutes or till a knife inserted near center comes out clean. Let stand 10 minutes before serving. Makes 6 servings.

Fruity Tofu Salad

1 lb fresh tofu
½ cup plain low-fat yogurt
½ tsp orange extract
1 package Equal
¼ cup reduced-calorie mayonnaise-type salad dressing
1 tsp curry powder
4 medium nectarines, sliced
1 cup of bias-sliced celery
lettuce leaves
¾ cup unsalted peanuts

Drain tofu by wrapping in a double thickness of cheese cloth or paper toweling. Press gently to extract as much moisture as possible. Cut into ½″ cubes. For dressing, combine yogurt, orange extract, Equal, salad dressing, and curry powder. Cover and chill in refrigerator for several hours. Meanwhile, arrange cubed tofu, nectarine slices, and celery on lettuce-lined plates. Spoon dressing over each salad. Top each salad with 3 Tbsp peanuts. Makes 4 servings.

Beef Barley Soup

½ lb stew meat
4 cups of homemade
  or canned beef
  broth
¼ cup barley
½ tsp basil

½ tsp salt (omit if
  canned broth is
  used)
1 cup thinly-sliced
  carrots
½ cup frozen baby
  lima beans
¼ cup chopped
  onion

Combine beef cubes and broth in Dutch oven or crock pot; bring to a boil. Add barley, basil and, if desired, salt. Cover; simmer 1 hour. Add vegetables; cover and continue cooking 15 to 20 minutes or until vegetables are tender. Makes four 1¼-cup servings.

Turkey Sausage Pita

¼ cup cooked,
   crumbled turkey
   sausage (see
   Fresh Breakfast
   Sausage recipe)
1 slice low-fat
   processed
   American cheese

1 whole-wheat mini
   pita round (3"
   diameter)
2 tomato slices
alfalfa sprouts
shredded lettuce

Slit pita round at one edge; open. Line pocket with cheese. Spoon turkey sausage mixture on top of cheese. Warm in oven or microwave to melt cheese. Top with sliced tomatoes, lettuce, and alfalfa sprouts as desired. Makes 1 pita sandwich.

Garden Chicken and Cheese Sandwich

1½ oz cooked sliced
   chicken breast
1 slice low-fat
   processed Swiss
   or ½ oz sliced
   mozzarella cheese
2 lettuce leaves
1 small tomato,
   sliced

¼ small cucumber,
   sliced
1 toasted whole-
   wheat English
   muffin
1 Tbsp low-calorie
   Italian or
   Thousand Island
   dressing

Layer chicken, cheese, lettuce, tomato, and cucumber on half of toasted muffin. Drizzle dressing between layers. Top with other half of toasted muffin.

Bulgur Salad Pita

⅓ cup bulgur wheat
¼ cup raisins
½ cup shredded carrot
½ cup plain low-fat yogurt

¼ cup slivered almonds, toasted
4 mini whole-wheat pita rounds (3″ diameter)
lettuce leaves

Combine bulgur and raisins. Add ⅔ cup cold water; let stand 1 hour or till bulgur is soft. Drain off any excess liquid. Stir in carrot. Cover and chill. Before serving, stir in yogurt and almonds. Slit open pita rounds at one edge. Line pita pockets with lettuce; spoon bulgur mixture into each. Serves 4.

Macaroni and Cheese

1½ cups elbow
  macaroni
  (enriched or whole
  wheat)
2 Tbsp margarine
2 Tbsp flour
½ tsp dry mustard
¼ tsp nutmeg
dash of pepper

2 cups skim milk
¼ cup finely
  chopped onion
8 oz low-fat cheddar-
  type cheese, cubed
  (try Weight
  Watcher's Natural
  or Fisher Country
  Charm)
1 tomato, sliced

Cook macaroni in boiling water till tender; drain. In saucepan, melt margarine; blend in flour, pepper, and mustard. Add milk; cook and stir till thick and bubbly. Add onion and cheese; stir till melted. Mix cheese sauce with macaroni and turn mixture into 1½-quart casserole. Arrange sliced tomato on top. Bake at 350° for 35 to 40 minutes. Makes 6 servings.

Kidney Bean Salad

2 cups cooked
   kidney beans
2/3 cup diced
   cucumber
1/2 cup diced celery
2 hard-cooked eggs,
   diced
1/4 tsp paprika

1/3 cup reduced-
   calorie
   mayonnaise-type
   salad dressing
1/8 tsp ground pepper
1/4 cup chopped
   onion

Mix all ingredients. Chill. Serves 6.

Supper Recipes

Beef Tacos

1 lb lean ground beef
1/2 cup chopped
   onion
1 clove garlic,
   minced
2 tsp chili powder
1 1/2 tsp vinegar
1 tsp ground cumin
1/8 tsp black pepper
1 tsp oregano,
   crushed

1/2 tsp salt (optional)
12 6" tortillas
6 oz low-fat
   processed
   American cheese
3 cups chopped
   tomato
shredded lettuce
taco sauce (optional)

184

Brown ground beef, onion, and garlic. Drain well. Absorb extra fat with paper towel. Add seasonings. Simmer 5 minutes. Warm tortillas in microwave or oven. Place ¼ cup meat mixture, ¼ cup chopped tomatoes, shredded lettuce, and ½ oz low-fat processed cheese in the center of each tortilla. If desired, shake on taco sauce. Fold tortilla around meat and vegetables. Makes 6 servings. Two tacos per serving.

Strawberry Tapioca Parfait

2½ cups skim milk
3 Tbsp quick
   cooking tapioca
3 Tbsp sugar
1 egg, beaten

1½ tsp vanilla
1¼ cups frozen or
   fresh sliced
   unsweetened
   strawberries
5 whole strawberries

In medium saucepan, combine milk, tapioca, sugar, and egg; let stand 5 minutes. Over medium heat, bring mixture to a boil, stirring constantly. Remove from heat; stir in vanilla. Let stand 10 minutes to cool and slightly thicken. In parfait glasses, alternate layers of pudding with sliced strawberries, ending with pudding. Refrigerate until ready to serve. Garnish with whole strawberries. Makes 5 servings.

Pan-Fried Fish

4 fish fillets, 3 oz
each
¼ cup low-cal Kraft
Zesty Italian
Dressing

Mrs. Dash, to taste
¼ cup Parmesan
cheese

Thaw fish in refrigerator; pat dry with paper towel. Baste fillets in Italian dressing. Sprinkle with Mrs. Dash. Pan fry in nonstick skillet until flaky. Be careful not to burn. Sprinkle Parmesan cheese on top. Cover and cook 2 minutes longer. Serves 4.

Pineapple Chicken Stir-Fry

1 can (8 oz) juice-
packed pineapple
chunks or tidbits
¼ lb fresh broccoli
1 Tbsp corn oil
½ cup diagonally
sliced carrots
¼ cup diagonally
sliced celery
1 small onion,
quartered
¼ tsp ground ginger

⅔ cup canned or
homemade
chicken broth
½ tsp salt (optional)
1 Tbsp soy sauce
1 Tbsp cornstarch
10 oz cooked cubed
chicken
3 cups hot cooked
brown rice

Drain pineapple; reserve juice. Separate broccoli into small flowerets; set aside. Cut stalk into thin slices. In 10″ nonstick skillet or fry pan over high heat, in hot oil, cook broccoli stalk slices, carrot, celery, and onion with ginger, stirring quickly and frequently until vegetables are crisp-tender. Add broccoli flowerets, stir-fry 1 minute more. In small bowl, combine reserved pineapple juice, broth, soy sauce and cornstarch; blend until smooth. Stir into vegetables. Reduce heat to medium high; cook, stirring constantly, until thickened. Add pineapple and chicken; heat thoroughly. Serve over rice. Makes 6 servings.

Spinach Rice Quiche

Crust:
2 cups cooked brown
    rice
1/4 cup egg substitute

1 Tbsp Parmesan
    cheese
dash garlic powder

Filling:
4 slices Swiss-
    flavored low-fat
    processed cheese
1 cup egg substitute
10 oz package
    chopped spinach,
    cooked and well
    drained

1/2 cup 2% cottage
    cheese
3 Tbsp Parmesan
    cheese
2 Tbsp skim milk
6 drops pepper sauce
1/4 tsp nutmeg

Preheat oven to 350°. Grease 9″ pie pan. In medium bowl beat ¼ cup egg substitute. Add rice and 1 Tbsp Parmesan cheese. Stir well. Add dash of garlic powder. Spread in pie pan. Arrange 4 low-fat cheese slices on rice crust. Beat 1 cup egg substitute. Stir in cottage cheese, Parmesan cheese, milk, spinach, pepper sauce, and nutmeg. Mix well. Pour into crust. Bake 35–45 minutes. Makes 5 servings.

Creamy Coleslaw

4 cups finely
    shredded cabbage
2 green onions,
    chopped,
    including tops
1 medium carrot,
    grated
¼ cup plain low-fat
    yogurt

¼ cup reduced-
    calorie
    mayonnaise-type
    salad dressing
2 Tbsp skim milk
1 Tbsp Dijon-style
    mustard
½ tsp celery seed
¼ tsp salt (optional)
dash pepper

Toss vegetables together until well mixed. Blend together yogurt, salad dressing, milk, mustard, celery seed, pepper and, if desired, salt. Toss vegetables with dressing mixture till well coated. Chill. Makes 8 servings.

Crispy Oven-Baked Chicken

½ cup grated
    Parmesan cheese
½ cup wheat germ
½ tsp dried
    rosemary
½ tsp onion powder
¼ tsp dried thyme

¼ tsp garlic powder
⅛ tsp pepper
¼ tsp salt (optional)
4 chicken breast
    halves, skinned
½ cup skim milk

Preheat oven to 325°. Lightly grease baking sheet. Combine all ingredients except chicken and milk. Dip chicken in milk, then roll in dry mixture and place on baking sheet. Bake until chicken tests done, about 50 to 60 minutes. Makes 4 servings.

Apple Crisp

6 medium cooking
    apples, peeled,
    cored, and sliced
1 Tbsp whole-wheat
    flour
¾ tsp cinnamon
¼ tsp ground
    nutmeg
¾ cup apple juice
¼ cup packed brown
    sugar
3 Tbsp whole-wheat
    flour

¼ tsp cinnamon
¼ tsp salt (optional)
¼ cup
    polyunsaturated
    margarine
½ cup quick or old-
    fashioned rolled
    oats, uncooked
3 Tbsp bran-type
    cereal or wheat
    germ
3 Tbsp chopped
    walnuts or pecans

In a bowl stir together apples, the 1 Tbsp flour, the ¾ tsp cinnamon, and the nutmeg. Turn into an 8 × 8 × 2″ baking dish, building up the edges slightly. Pour apple juice over the fruit. In another bowl combine brown sugar, the remaining flour, the 1 tsp cinnamon, and the salt. Cut in margarine until well blended. Stir in remaining ingredients. Sprinkle over fruit in center, leaving a ring of apples showing around the edge. Bake at 375° for 30 minutes. Makes 12 servings.

Zesty Spinach Lasagna

2 10-oz packages frozen chopped spinach, cooked and drained
¼ tsp garlic powder
2 Tbsp parsley flakes
1½ Tbsp basil
3 cups canned tomatoes
2 6-oz cans tomato paste
2 tsp sugar
1 tsp oregano

8 oz lasagna noodles, enriched or whole wheat
3 cups 2% cottage cheese
2 eggs, beaten
1 tsp pepper
3 Tbsp parsley flakes
½ cup Parmesan cheese
12 oz mozzarella cheese, grated

Combine spinach with next 7 ingredients. Simmer uncovered until sauce is thick (45 to 60 minutes). Cook noodles in boiling water till tender; drain; rinse in cold water. Meanwhile combine cottage cheese with eggs, seasonings, and Parmesan cheese. Place half of the cooked noodles in a 13 × 9" baking dish; spread half the cottage cheese mixture over noodles; sprinkle half the mozzarella cheese; spoon on half the spinach mixture. Repeat layers. Sprinkle top lightly with Parmesan cheese. Bake at 350° for 30 to 40 minutes. Let stand 15 minutes; cut in squares. Makes 12 servings.

Baked Apples

4 baking apples
1/4 cup raisins
1/4 cup unsweetened
   apple juice
   concentrate

3/4 tsp ground
   cinnamon
1/8 tsp ground
   nutmeg

Wash and core apples. Place in a flat baking dish. Combine raisins, apple juice concentrate, cinnamon, and nutmeg. Mix well. Stuff cores of apples with mixture. Bake uncovered in 350° oven for 25 to 35 minutes. Baste apples occasionally with pan liquids while baking. Makes 4 servings.

Lemon-Herb Broiled Chicken

4 chicken breast
    halves, skinned
    and pierced with
    a fork
3 Tbsp lemon juice
2 Tbsp corn oil

½ tsp rosemary
    leaves, crushed
¼ tsp thyme leaves
⅛ tsp garlic powder
dash pepper
dash paprika
¼ tsp salt (optional)

Arrange chicken bone side up on broiler pan. In small bowl combine remaining ingredients; brush over chicken. Broil about 4 inches from heat for 8 minutes, brushing frequently with sauce. Turn chicken; continue broiling, brushing frequently with sauce, for 6 to 8 minutes or until chicken is tender. Makes 4 servings.

Bulgur Pilaf

1 cup bulgur wheat,
    uncooked
1 tsp margarine
¼ cup chopped
    onion
¼ cup thinly sliced
    celery

2 cups homemade or
    canned chicken
    broth
¼ tsp oregano
dash pepper
⅛ tsp salt (omit if
    canned broth is
    used)

Melt margarine in skillet. Add bulgur, onion, and celery. Stir and cook till golden. Add broth and seasonings. Cover and bring to a boil. Reduce heat and simmer 15 minutes. Makes 4 ½-cup servings.

Scandinavian Baked Fish

1 lb package frozen
  fish fillets
¼ cup chopped
  onion
¼ cup chopped
  celery
¼ cup chopped green
  pepper
1 Tbsp margarine

1 small tomato,
  peeled and
  chopped
1 Tbsp parsley
1 Tbsp lemon juice
½ tsp dried dill weed
¼ tsp salt (optional)

Allow fish to stand unwrapped at room temperature for 20 minutes. Bias slice fish into 1-inch slices. In saucepan cook onion, celery, and green pepper in margarine till tender. Stir in tomato, parsley, lemon juice, and dill weed. Arrange fish slices overlapping slightly in an ungreased baking dish. Spoon vegetable mixture over fish. Bake uncovered in 450° oven for 18 to 20 minutes or till fish flakes easily. Makes 6 servings.

Curried Chicken over Rice

½ cup chopped
onion
1 Tbsp oil
3 Tbsp flour
¼ tsp salt (optional)
1½ cups cooked,
cubed chicken
1 cup homemade or
canned chicken
broth

¾ cup skim milk
1 tart red apple,
cored, chopped
½ tsp curry powder
¼ tsp ginger
3 cups cooked brown
rice
¼ cup slivered
almonds
2 Tbsp raisins

In large skillet, cook onion in oil till tender. Stir in flour; add chicken, broth, milk, apple, curry powder, and ginger. Simmer, stirring frequently 5 to 7 minutes or till mixture is thickened. Serve over hot rice; sprinkle with almonds and raisins. Makes 6 servings.

Healthy Cookies

¾ cup whole-wheat
flour
¼ cup unprocessed
bran
¼ cup nonfat dry
milk
½ tsp salt (optional)
½ tsp baking powder
½ tsp baking soda
½ cup margarine
½ cup peanut butter

½ cup honey
2 eggs
1 tsp vanilla
½ cup raisins
1 cup dried apricots,
chopped
¾ cup rolled oats
⅓ cup unsalted
sunflower seeds

Stir together flour, unprocessed bran, milk powder, baking powder, and baking soda. In large mixing bowl beat together margarine, peanut butter, and honey. Add egg and vanilla, mixing well. Combine remaining ingredients with flour mixture and then add to peanut butter mixture. Blend well. Drop by rounded teaspoonsful onto an ungreased cookie sheet. Bake in 350° oven for 10 to 11 minutes. Let cool on cookie sheet for 1 minute. Remove to wire rack to cool completely. Makes 4½ to 5½ dozen cookies.

Favorite Meat Loaf

1 lb lean ground beef
1 lb fresh or frozen
   ground turkey
2 eggs or 1 cup egg
   substitute
1 cup rolled oats
½ cup parsley
2 Tbsp chopped
   chives or onion

1 Tbsp dried basil
½ Tbsp dried dill
   weed
¼ tsp salt (optional)
½ tsp pepper
1 cup tomato sauce
   or tomato juice

Combine all ingredients and mix well. Shape into loaf in pie pan or cookie sheet. Bake 1½ hours at 350°. Serves 8.

Tabouli, Bean, and Cheese Casserole

1¼ cups bulgur
   wheat, uncooked
4 cups boiling water
1 cup red beans,
   cooked
1½ cups fresh
   minced parsley
¾ cup chopped green
   onions

2–3 medium fresh
   tomatoes, chopped
2 Tbsp lemon juice
1 Tbsp oil
2 oz cheddar cheese,
   grated
taco sauce to taste

Combine bulgur wheat and boiling water and let stand several hours or overnight. Drain excess water. Mix bulgur with remaining ingredients in casserole. Bake at 350° for ½ hour. Top with grated cheddar cheese and heat to melt cheese. Makes 6 servings.

Turkey Meatball Sandwich

Meatballs:
1 lb fresh or frozen
  ground turkey
½ cup fine dry bread
  crumbs
¼ cup grated
  Parmesan cheese
2 Tbsp dried parsley
¼ cup egg substitute
1½ tsp dried
  oregano
1½ tsp dried basil

Sauce:
1 large can whole
  tomatoes
6-oz can tomato
  paste
½ cup chopped
  onion
½ cup chopped green
  pepper
1 cup fresh
  mushrooms
1 garlic clove,
  minced
2 tsp sugar

Mix first 5 ingredients, ½ tsp oregano, and ½ tsp basil. Shape into 1-inch meatballs (about 24). Sauté in non-stick skillet over medium heat until browned and no longer pink. Add all remaining ingredients to pan and bring to a boil. Simmer covered until sauce is thickened, about 30 minutes. Serve 2 meatballs with ¼-cup sauce in hard roll.

Pumpkin Custard

1 cup canned
   pumpkin
1 cup evaporated
   skimmed milk
⅓ cup brown sugar
1 egg

¾ tsp cinnamon
¼ tsp ginger
⅛ tsp cloves
¼ tsp nutmeg

Mix ingredients together. Stir well. Pour into 4 custard cups; set cups in shallow pan on oven rack. Pour hot water into pan, 1-inch deep. Bake at 325° for 40 to 45 minutes, or until knife inserted comes out clean. Serve warm or chilled.

Pantry Particulars

The following grocery list includes all foods needed for the various recipes and menus provided. Keep the items listed in the "staples" category in stock at all times. Be sure to check what you already have on hand. The quantity purchased will depend on the number of people eating. Substitutes may need to be made with fruits and vegetables depending on what is in season and on personal preferences.

Staples

Whole wheat flour
White flour
Baking soda
Baking powder
Cornstarch
Quick cooking tapioca
Granulated sugar
Brown sugar
Honey
Molasses
Mrs. Dash
Ground cinnamon
Dried parsley
Rubbed sage
Paprika
Onion powder
Garlic powder
Thyme
Fennel seed
Black pepper
Salt
Celery seed
Chili powder
Bay leaves
Marjoram

Pickling spices
Dried dill weed
Dried basil
Curry powder
Dry mustard
Ground nutmeg
Ground cumin
Dried leaf oregano
Ground ginger
Rosemary
Ground cloves
Vanilla extract
Orange extract
Almond extract
Lemon extract
Equal
Cider vinegar
Dijon-style mustard
Tabasco sauce
Taco sauce
Soy sauce
Canned beef broth
Canned chicken broth
Diet lime gelatin

Dairy Products

Skim milk
Plain low-fat yogurt
Lemon low-fat yogurt
Neufchatel cream
   cheese

Low-fat processed
   American cheese
   slices
Low-fat processed
   Swiss cheese
   slices

2% milk fat cottage cheese

Grated Parmesan cheese

Low-fat cheddar-type cheese (try Weight Watcher's Natural or Fisher Country Charm)

Farmer's cheese

Part skim mozzarella cheese

Sugar-free cocoa

Nonfat dry milk powder

Evaporated skimmed milk

Grain Products

Rolled oats

Bran flakes

Unprocessed bran

Bulgur

Wheat germ

Whole-wheat bagels

Hard rolls

Whole-wheat bread

Whole-wheat English muffins

Whole grain crackers (try Rye Krisp or Ak-Mak)

Mini whole-wheat pita bread (3″ diameter)

Corn tortillas

Brown rice

Corkscrew pasta, enriched or whole wheat

Elbow macaroni, enriched or whole wheat

Lasagna noodles, enriched or whole wheat

Fruits and Vegetables

Apples

Baking apples

Cantaloupe

Bananas

Oranges

Grapefruit

Grapes

Pears

Nectarines or peaches
Plums
Fresh or frozen
unsweetened
strawberries
Fresh carrots
Green pepper
Fresh tomatoes
Celery
Alfalfa sprouts
Baking potatoes
Fresh broccoli
Fresh mushrooms
Onions
Green onions
Garlic
Lettuce
Cucumber
Cabbage
Fresh spinach
Fresh parsley
Fresh yams
Fresh cauliflower
Frozen orange juice
concentrate
Frozen apple juice
concentrate
Frozen baby lima
beans
Frozen peas
Frozen mixed
vegetables

Frozen spinach
Frozen kernel corn
Juice-packed canned
peaches
Juice-packed canned
pineapple tidbits
Unsweetened canned
applesauce
Juice-packed canned
fruit cocktail
Juice-packed canned
bing cherries
Juice-packed canned
pears
Tomato paste
Canned whole
tomatoes
Canned green beans
Canned wax beans
Pimiento
Canned beets
Tomato juice
Low-salt spaghetti
sauce
Lemon juice
concentrate
Stewed tomatoes
Canned pumpkin
Raisins
Dried apricots

Protein Foods

Eggs
Fresh or frozen ground
 turkey
Turkey breast
Chicken breast
85% lean ground beef
Frozen egg substitute
Stew meat
Pork chops, center cut
Tofu

Peanut butter
Water-packed canned
 tuna
Canned chili-style
 beans
Red beans
Garbanzo beans
Lentils
Kidney beans

Fats and Oils

Corn oil margarine
Corn oil
Kraft Zesty Italian
 Reduced-Calorie
 Dressing
Reduced-calorie
 mayonnaise-type
 salad dressing (try
 Miracle Whip
 Light)

Low-calorie Thousand
 Island Dressing
Slivered almonds
Chopped nuts
Unsalted sunflower
 seeds
Unsalted peanuts

Some Suggestions

1. Eat breakfast. It really is important. Many people don't because they aren't hungry. Exercising in the morning will stimulate the appetite.
2. Drink water. Water is a neglected liquid. It's still the cheapest, lowest calorie beverage and is good for you, too.

3. Avoid eating between meals. This is usually a sign of boredom, not hunger, and can cause weight problems. Being overweight causes more burden on joints. Eating three meals a day will take care of hunger. Eating for any other reason is a problem.

4. Be aware of what you eat to the point of writing it down. "I ate five cream puffs today" tends to slap you in the face when you look at it in black and white. Otherwise, the cream puffs may slide by unnoticed (until they show up in expanding skin).

5. Try not to think about food. That's hard since it's everywhere you look—TV, magazines, even billboards. When you find yourself thinking about it, think of something else—goals, tasks, even arthritis—or do something else. Hug your kid, exercise, get involved in a task.

6. Don't be too hard on yourself. We are all human, and if eating is something you enjoy, at least don't be too compulsive about it. That in itself can cause stress. The important thing is the long haul. If you do what you're supposed to do most of the time, you can afford to splurge once in a while. When you do, enjoy!

10 Sex and Arthritis

⚄⚄⚄⚄

One thing about arthritis is that it is always around and is not shy about lurking in its victim's bedroom. It won't just leave the room, the proper and courteous thing to do. In fact, the bedroom may possibly be one of the most annoying places that it makes its presence felt. It can be a real nuisance, showing up at very intimate moments and causing embarrassment and frustration. Talking about arthritis, not ignoring it, will make its interference easier to deal with.

Communication is an overused word when talking about arthritis, but its importance cannot be stressed enough. While you may have established a good relationship with your doctor, the communication will probably stop at the subject of sex. This communication must then be redirected to your partner. Talking can enhance anyone's sex life, but it is essential for those who must deal with arthritis and sex. Many problems are relatively easy to deal with if you communicate. For instance, you may feel less attractive because of your arthritis. Your partner, on the other hand, may be reluctant to have sex for fear of hurting you. If these thoughts are not expressed, you may interpret your partner's reluctance as proof of your unattractiveness. Your partner needs to reassure you, and you need to let your partner know what hurts so adjustments can be made.

Your sex drive may decrease, and you need to make your partner aware that this is no indication of your lack of desire for him or her. It may simply be a side effect of your disease or possibly of the medication you are taking. Just as you need reassurance, your partner needs reassurance. It is important to avoid hurt feelings as well as physical hurt. Feelings not expressed physically can be expressed through words.

Generally, there is no reason why people with arthritis cannot have satisfying sex lives. By experimenting with different positions, (and experimenting can be fun), you can discover the positions that are the most comfortable. It may help to take a warm bath before sex to relax and to take your medication so that it will work at the time you plan to have sex. Try to get some rest during the day so you can avoid excessive fatigue at night.

These are a few specific suggestions, but a successful sex life depends primarily on you and your partner's ability to communicate. If you didn't talk about sex before, you will need to start. You may even be pleasantly surprised and find that your sex life is better than ever. Arthritis will still be there, but if you talk about it its presence will seem less and less important.

11 Working with Arthritis

೫೫೫೫

To work with arthritis means to work with it as well as *cooperate* with it. Arthritis will not leave you alone for a designated eight hours a day and let you do your job. It tags along, interfering, interrupting, and demanding your attention. But you are a busy person, and you cannot take a permanent vacation just because arthritis has moved in. Some adjustments may be necessary, and you may have more than your share of compromises. Working with arthritis means establishing a new set of rules for success.

Set up a Have To/Should Do/Want To schedule for work as well. Coffee breaks were invented because people need to take breaks. Instead of pumping up on caffeine, which can make you feel more stressed, do some relaxation exercises, or read something you want to, or go for a walk around the building if it's a nice day. If you have a good relationship with your employer, pass it on. It can do wonders for the boss as well as for co-workers and can result in quality production. After all, seven hours of quality time can be more productive than eight hours spent racing through a job under stress. These suggestions can help anyone, but if you have arthritis your needs may be special.

Depending on the type and severity of your arthritis, your adjustments can range from minor to drastic. Minor adjustments may be all you need—a new chair or desk, or more flexibility in movement to prevent stiffness. You may need to talk to your employer. Ideally, the employer is understanding, but this is not always the case. You may have to request a different, more suitable position within the company before the need is apparent. Perhaps working a different shift, the time during which you usually feel best, would help.

You may require temporary disability while your disease is brought under control. Fortunately, with proper treatment most people are not permanently disabled. If you must go on temporary disability, you may have to seek new employment following treatment. The Division of Vocational Rehabilitation tests your strengths and weaknesses, and the State Employment Service will take special steps to place you in a position that suits your capabilities.

Most drastically, you may not be able to work at all because of the severity of your disease. This is rare, but in some cases it may be mandatory. Contact the

Social Security office or your local Arthritis Foundation chapter for information and instructions on benefits for which you qualify.

Household and personal responsibilities are always present. Again, adjustments can range from minor to drastic. You should avoid doing any one household task for a long time. You may need to purchase devices to help you with routine tasks, such as grab bars for the tub, or fat-handled silverware. Keep frequently-used items in accessible locations so you aren't constantly bending and stooping. Raising the bed can make for more graceful entrances and exits. There are devices designed to help you dress yourself. Occupational therapists are available at most hospitals. Their job is to instruct you and your family members in the use of devices as well as giving you helpful hints for coping with arthritis.

Finally, you may require outside help with domestic chores. Visiting nurses, physical therapists, and housekeepers may be needed on a part-time or full-time basis. Your using such help depends on your financial situation.

Here you are, worried about your ability to perform your job while arthritis costs you even more money. You may qualify for financial aid. Find out what help is available by contacting your local Arthritis Foundation chapter. Your best source of information about anything and everything concerning arthritis is the Arthritis Foundation. They are willing and able to answer your questions. Providing services for people with arthritis is the reason the foundation exists.

Arthritis may cramp your style, but working with it means working *with* it. The degree of cooperation depends on the severity of its intrusion. Working with arthritis, like living with it, demands flexibility on your part. Give in when necessary, rebel when possible, and seek help when available. Fortunately, with proper treatment and help from the family, friends, and community services, most people with arthritis can continue to work and be very successful.

12 A Joint Venture: Arthritis and You

ನಣನಣ

Besides the obvious pun, a joint venture means living your life with your new, constant companion, arthritis. Arthritis is a very real part of you. It moves in with the nicest people and then becomes part of their personality. Arthritis is the nasty side—the grouchy, complaining, uncooperative side that threatens to control the nice person with whom it moves in. Let's face it; no one wants to be around such a person, least of all you, but you don't have the luxury of walking away from it. Other people are sympathetic but not empathetic, and it is a great burden for you to be nice with arthritis forever in the way.

When arthritis moves in, it brings with it many negative aspects. It brings despair and makes you desperate. It brings depression and depresses your thoughts and actions. It brings anger, and the anger is contagious. It brings pessimism that drowns your optimism. Arthritis is frustration, embarrassment, and resentment; a financial drain and an emotional strain. It is worry, guilt, and self pity, but above all else it is pain.

All of these traits become part of your personality, and it is a constant battle to subdue the arthritis side, the negative characteristics, and maintain a positive attitude. In the face of all this adversity—you do it! You lead a normal life. When you think about it that way, you really do deserve a pat on the back. You aren't proud that arthritis lives with you, but you have every reason to be proud of your ability to deal with it. You truly deserve to be recognized as a remarkable person. Most people can tolerate pain for a short time, but it is a special person who can tolerate chronic pain and remain a nice person. If you have negative feelings, don't feel guilty about it. Those feelings are part of the arthritis that is part of you. Arthritis tests the stamina of the very strongest, and the fact that you deal with it at all is evidence that you are strong. It's a heavy responsibility, but because you are strong you will deal with it and win control.

Life with arthritis does not have to be a miserable existence. True, living with arthritis requires patience beyond that of living with the worst roommate imaginable, but with willpower and patience you and arthritis can live in a peaceful coexistence.

People with arthritis must be patient patients. Living with arthritis requires the patience of a martyr, and dealing with chronic pain makes you a martyr of sorts. Arthritis may be determined to rule your roost, but it is up to you to take charge and remain in control. Research continues daily, but until there is a cure, it is up to you to keep arthritis in line.

First, accept arthritis. Ignoring it will not make it go away. In fact, arthritis thrives on ignoring and ignorance. You should learn as much as possible about it. Educating yourself about arthritis helps you deal with it. By understanding the disease you can understand proper treatment, and you will be less likely to fall victim to quackery. You won't waste valuable time and money on unproven remedies, and you can get on with the business of controlling your arthritis with the help of medical science. If you are tempted to try a new "cure" (and you will be), ask your doctor. A good relationship with a doctor can contribute to your success in controlling arthritis. The joint venture, then, also includes you and your doctor. If you cannot talk openly with your doctor, find one with whom you can. The doctor can do only as much as you can do for yourself. He cannot read your mind. Questions that are never asked can never be answered. If you are intimidated by a doctor, it will be you who loses, not the doctor. Sharing thoughts, concerns, and symptoms helps the doctor prescribe what is best for you. He or she may need to try several medications, and the patient patient must hang in there until the right one is found. Follow the doctor's instructions on rest, exercise, diet, and medication. It won't be a picnic, but it will pay off in the long run.

Whenever possible, educate your family about arthritis. Loved ones need to be aware that you do not have arthritis by choice. Your family, too, can be part of your joint venture. You may need to be patient with them to get them on your side. Try to keep the arthritis side, the negative side, in check. Others will not always appreciate this, but you must do it for yourself as well as to gain family support. Express your unhappiness with your burden, not by complaining but by educating. By understanding the disease, loved ones will come to understand that the pain is very real and very unpredictable, that you are not faking it when one minute you feel fine and the next awful. As they learn about arthritis, they will gain a sense of what you put up with and respect for you. To have the support and understanding of loved ones will help you deal with your arthritis intrusion. Finally, friends can also become part of your joint venture. If misery loves company, then arthritis is the perfect companion. Talking with someone else who has arthritis can make you feel better. You'll realize that you are not alone in your misery.

In fact, you have more friends willing and able to help than you are aware of. You share a friend with 36 million other people in the form of the Arthritis Foundation. The Arthritis Foundation exists for your benefit. The address of state and local chapters can be found in the phone book. If you have difficulty locating a local chapter, contact the national chapter at Arthritis Foundation, 3400 Peachtree Road, N.E., Atlanta, Georgia 30326. They will be able to direct you to the chapter nearest you. The Arthritis Foundation will counsel, recommend physicians, and give information about support groups as well as many social services for which you might qualify. They publish pamphlets that discuss in more detail some of the aspects of arthritis covered in this book. Have your family read these pamphlets. They are an excellent source of information about arthritis. The pamphlets are free and are available in most doctors' offices or through your local Arthritis Foundation chapter.

You are not alone, and people will help you if you ask. Remember that seeking help does not mean you are helpless. You should help yourself as much as possible for your own self esteem. But you do not help yourself much by trying to force a task that would be easily accomplished if you simply asked for a little help. When you need help, put yourself in the other person's place. If they asked *you* to do the same thing, would you refuse? More than likely, you would be happy to do it and not give it another thought. Give others credit for having the same consideration. Family, friends, your doctor, and the Arthritis Foundation can all be part of your joint venture with arthritis.

Ultimately, though, the joint venture is you and your arthritis. Controlling arthritis means that it does not take over your life. Arthritis, characteristically, has the tendency to do just that. There is little question that arthritis alters your life-style, perhaps drastically, but you are the one who controls your life-style. Controlling arthritis will keep you on your toes, but consider it a challenge. If arthritis wins too many battles, you may lose the war. So set small and achievable goals, so that you win on a daily basis. To control arthritis and achieve the highest degree of health of which you are capable, you will need to establish a routine that promotes health.

Your physical routine will include proper diet, exercise, rest, and medication. Your mental routine will involve reducing stress and working on a positive attitude. Controlling arthritis begins with your attitude toward arthritis. Perhaps the single most important aspect discussed in this book is your attitude. Your wanting to control arthritis is the first step. This attitude will give you the determination to follow through with subsequent steps to achieve this goal.

The ace that you hold is controlling the effect arthritis has on your mind. Arthritis has moved into your body and will never again be the last thing on your mind. You can see to it that it is not the *only* thing on your mind.

PHASE THREE

≈≈≈≈

The Arthritis Workbook

You've read through Phases One and Two; you're done, right? Wrong. There is still Phase Three. You may have learned a great deal, but all of this knowledge means nothing if you don't do something with it. Now is the time to practice some of these principles. Following are examples of a workbook for you to complete every day. A workbook suggests that you have some work to do. If you really want to help yourself control arthritis, there will be some work. But anything worthwhile is worth working for, and it will take some effort on your part to take time each day to fill out the workbook and accomplish those goals. The time you spend planning in the morning and evaluating at night is time to spend on yourself. It is valuable time that will help you put things in perspective and keep you aware of your activities and thoughts. You can fill out your workbook in as much detail as you like. At the very least, the workbook will help keep you organized and serve as a record for appointments and activities.

The workbook incorporates many things discussed in the book. In the morning, you should fill out the Have To, Should Do, and Want To columns as well as what you intend to do for yourself physically, emotionally, and intellectually. At the end of the day, you will put check marks beside what you have accomplished. Remember that *nothing* in the Should Do column should be checked on any given day. Move that task over into the Have To column the next day. You should also fill out what medications were taken and when. Did you think of any important questions that you would like to ask your doctor on your next visit? Write them down. Did you exercise? How and for how long? Write down what you ate that day. Rate your pain and stiffness on a scale of 1–10, with 10 being the most pain or the most stiffness. Rating pain and stiffness can help chart trends of your disease. Finally, evaluate your day. Did you accomplish what you set out to do? If not, why? How do you feel about that?

After about six weeks, go back and reassess things. Did you get to do what you wanted to for the most part? If not, why not? Do you feel less or more under stress? Why? Did you exercise and eat correctly most of the time? Does there seem to be a more appropriate time to take your medications? How did your ratings of pain and stiffness seem to correlate with the kind of day you had? Read your journal. That can be fun as well as give you insight into what you may be doing right or wrong.

It is also a good idea to do this type of reassessing before you visit your doctor. You can tell your doctor what you are doing and ask necessary questions. This can only enhance patient/doctor communication and therefore enhance your doctor's ability to help you.

We have included two weeks worth of workbook to help you establish the format. Following the two weeks, buy a pad of Big Chief, or any other notebook, and keep going. Hopefully, this will become a lifelong ritual whether you actually write it down or not, but at least give the system six weeks, minimum, to see results. The longer you have neglected yourself, the longer it will take to begin feeling healthier. Generally, though, you should notice improvement in about six weeks. If so, keep going. If the system doesn't work, then you are back at square one and need to search for something that does. There will be no harm done in trying this system. The first three pages of the workbook have been filled in as examples to help you get started. Good luck!

Date _Friday_

What I Hope to Accomplish

Have To	Should Do	Want To
Go to work ✓	laundry	visit my sister ✓
pay bills ✓	get groceries	read ✓
pick up Joey at school ✓	clean house	
go to dentist ✓	wash car	
	clean out underwear drawer	
	work on yard	

What I Will Do for Myself

Physical	Emotional	Intellectual
shower ✓	talk to Joey ✓	read ✓
floss teeth ✓		

Medications Taken

Drug	Amount	Time(s)
aspirin	3	7 AM.
	3	noon
	3	6 p.m.
	3	10 p.m

Things to Tell or Ask Doctor

Exercise

morning routine
did some relaxation at work

Nutrition

Breakfast	Lunch	Supper	Snacks
bran flakes wheat toast banana orange juice coffee	skipped (an apple later in after- noon)	fish baked potato peas peaches milk	

Daily Rating (1–10) Pain 4   Stiffness 2

Journal

Had a pretty good day Stopped by my sister's
for a while after picking up Joey Had a nice
talk with Joey on the way home I skipped lunch
because of my appointment No cavities!

Date *Saturday*

What I Hope to Accomplish

Have To	Should Do	Want To
get groceries ✓	wash car	nap
do laundry ✓	clean out under-	call Sue ✓
clean house ✓	wear drawer	play with Joey ✓
mow yard ✓	bake some goodies	
hair appointments	sew and mend	
	clothes	

What I Will Do for Myself

Physical	Emotional	Intellectual
shower ✓	play with Joey ✓	read paper ✓
get hair cut ✓	spend time with	do crossword puzzle
	spouse ✓	(Did partially)

Medications Taken

Drug	Amount	Time(s)
aspirin	3	7 am
	3	noon
	3	6 pm
	3	10 pm
Tylenol	2	3:30 pm

Things to Tell or Ask Doctor

Is it OK to take Tylenol with aspirin?

Exercise
just housework and yardwork

Nutrition

Breakfast	Lunch	Supper	Snacks
pancakes with strawberry sauce milk coffee	chicken and cheese sandwich pear milk	pizza decaffeinated cola	

Daily Rating (1–10) Pain   6   Stiffness   3

Journal

Had an extremely busy day, but feel pretty good—got a lot done. Had a headache in the afternoon and took some Tylenol. Enjoyed visiting with Sue, didn't have time for a nap—will go to bed early. Played with Joey after doing yardwork. He was really tired, so we fed him early and put him to bed. Spouse and I treated ourselves to takeout pizza—alone! Really like my hair

Date *Sunday*

What I Hope to Accomplish

Have To	Should Do	Want To
church ✓ wash car ✓	clean out underwear drawer sew and mend clothes write letters	sleep in ✓ read Sunday paper ✓ nap ✓ picnic ✓

What I Will Do for Myself

Physical	Emotional	Intellectual
take a long hot bath ✓	spend time with spouse and Joy ✓	read ✓

Medications Taken		
Drug	Amount	Time(s)
aspirin	3 3 3 3	9:00 a m 1:00 p m 6:30 p m 10:30 p m

Things to Tell or Ask Doctor

Exercise

did morning routine
went for a walk

Nutrition

Breakfast	Lunch	Supper	Snacks
	BRUNCH	chicken	snack in
eggs, sausage, toast,		rice	afternoon
strawberries, orange juice		vegetable salad	vegetables &
coffee		angel food cake	dip
		milk	

Daily Rating (1–10) Pain 4   **Stiffness** 2

Journal

Terrific day! Slept in a little – went to later church services. Fixed fantastic brunch that we devoured. Washed the car, and went for a little walk. Took a long bath while I read the paper. We all took a short nap and had a little picnic afterwards. I feel so good, I may actually clean out my underwear drawer before I go to bed . nah!

Before You Begin

Doing this workbook shows that you are ready to be responsible for yourself. But it is a choice. You can do it or not do it; you can cheat or be honest. It's up to you. If you see it as a joke and write down a "trip to the Bahamas" under your Want To column, then obviously you are being unrealistic, and it probably will not work for you. That's okay. It will not work for everyone. But if you don't try this method or any other method to help yourself, you are shirking your responsibility for your health and on your way to becoming a negative person. Others do not want to be around negative people. We all cheer for the underdog, the person who perseveres and succeeds under adversity. We see it in movies and read about it in books. We admire those people, cheer them on, and call them courageous. Your life story is not likely to be made into a Movie of the Week, but you can create your own cheering section of family and friends if you have a good attitude. What do you have to lose? You just may cut arthritis down to size. Give it your best shot!

Pronunciation Key

✿✿✿✿

acetaminophen   (as"e-tuh-mee'no-fen)
allopurinol   (al"o-pew'ri-nol)
amitriptyline   (am"i-trip'ti-leen)
ankylosing spondylitis   (ank'i-loaz-ing spon"di-lye'tis)
arthroplasty   (ahr'thro-plas"tee)
arthroscopy   (ahr-thros'kuh-pee)
azathioprine   (az"uh-thigh'o-preen)

betamethasone   (bay"tuh-meth'uh-sone)
bursitis   (bur-sigh'tis)

chlorambucil   (klor-am'bew-sil)
cimetidine   (sim"e-tigh'deen)
codeine   (ko'deen)
colchicine   (kol'chi-seen)

corticosteroid   (kor"ti-ko-steer'oyd)
cortisone   (kor'ti-sone)
creatinine   (kree-at'i-neen)
crepitus   (krep'i-tus)
cyclophosphamide   (sigh"klo-fos'fuh-mide)

dermatomyositis   (dur"muh-toe-migh-o-sigh'tis)
dexamethasone   (deck"suh-meth'uh-sone)
dimethyl sulfoxide   (dye-meth'il sulf-ock'side)
D-penicillamine   (dee-pen"i-sil'uh-meen)

erythrocyte   (e-rith'ro-sight)

fibromyalgia   (figh"bro-migh-al'juh)
fibrositis   (figh"bro-sigh'tis)
fluocinolone   (floo"o-sin'uh-lohn)

gout   (gowt)

hydroxychloroquine   (high-drock"see-klo'ro-kween)

ibuprofen   (eye-bew'pro-fen)
indomethacin   (in"do-meth'uh-sin)

lupus   erythematosus   (lew'pus   err'i-theem"uh-to'sus)

meclofenamate   (meck"lo-fen'uh-mate)
methotrexate   (meth"o-treck'sate)
metoclopramide   (met"o-klo-pram'ide)

Pronunciation Key

osteoarthritis (os"tee-o-ahr-thrigh'tis)
osteoporosis (os"tee-o-po-ro'sis)
oxyphenbutazone (ock"si-fen-bew'tuh-zone)

phenylbutazone (fen"il-bew'tuh-zone)
plasmapheresis (plaz"muh-ferr'e-sis)
polyarteritis nodosa (pol"ee-ahr"te-rye'tis no-do'suh)
polymyalgia rheumatica (pol"ee-migh-al'jee-uh roo-mat'i-kuh)
polymyositiş (pol"ee-migh-o-sigh'tis)
prednisolone (pred-nis'uh-lohn)
prednisone (pred'ni-sohn)
probenecid (pro-ben'e-sid)
propoxyphene (pro-pock'see-feen)
pseudogout (sue"do-gowt')
psoriasis (so-rye'uh-sis)

ranitidine (ran"i-tigh'deen)
Raynaud's phenomenon (ray-noz')
Reiter's syndrome (right'erz)
Reye's syndrome (rise)
rheumatoid (roo'muh-toyd)

salicylate (sa-lis'-i-late)
scleroderma (skleer"o-dur'muh)
Sjogren's syndrome (show'grens)
synovectomy (sin"o-veck'tuh-mee)
synovitis (sin"o-vye'tis)

temporal arteritis   (tem'puh-rul ahr"te-rye'tis)
tendinitis   (ten"duh-nigh'tis)
titer   (tye'tur)
triamcinolone   (trye"am-sin'o-lone)

uric   (yoor'ick)
vasculitis   (vas"kew-lye'tis)

Afterword

ಸಿಸಿಸಿ

We talk a lot about the importance of support groups. Maybe you are many miles from a city that offers water exercise programs or has established support groups. Maybe your nearest Arthritis Foundation chapter is a hundred miles away. You may feel isolated and alone. But remember, arthritis affects one in seven people, and the chances are that you know at least one other person who has arthritis. Form a support group of two. There is no minimum requirement. Get together with this person and talk, share "gripe time," and exercise together. That's really what a support group is all about: sharing, working together, solving problems—friendship. Make a point of meeting at each other's house once a week. Who knows? Maybe you could really start something in your area. You never know who might show up. But one thing is for sure—arthritis will be there.

Date

What I Hope to Accomplish

Have To	Should Do	Want To

What I Will Do for Myself

Physical	Emotional	Intellectual

	Medications Taken	
Drug	*Amount*	*Time(s)*

Things to Tell or Ask Doctor

234

Exercise

Nutrition

Breakfast	Lunch	Supper	Snacks

Daily Rating (1–10) Pain _____ Stiffness _____

Journal

Date

What I Hope to Accomplish

Have To	Should Do	Want To

What I Will Do for Myself

Physical	Emotional	Intellectual

Medications Taken

Drug	Amount	Time(s)

Things to Tell or Ask Doctor

		Exercise		

		Nutrition		
Breakfast	*Lunch*	*Supper*	*Snacks*

Daily Rating (1–10) Pain _____ **Stiffness** _____

Journal

Exercise			

Nutrition			
Breakfast	*Lunch*	*Supper*	*Snacks*

Daily Rating (1–10) Pain _____ Stiffness _____

Journal _____

	Exercise		

	Nutrition		
Breakfast	*Lunch*	*Supper*	*Snacks*

Daily Rating (1–10) Pain _____   Stiffness _____

Journal

Date

What I Hope to Accomplish

Have To	Should Do	Want To

What I Will Do for Myself

Physical	Emotional	Intellectual

Medications Taken		
Drug	*Amount*	*Time(s)*

Things to Tell or Ask Doctor

Exercise			

Nutrition

Breakfast	Lunch	Supper	Snacks

Daily Rating (1–10) Pain _____ Stiffness _____

Journal

Date

What I Hope to Accomplish

Have To	Should Do	Want To

What I Will Do for Myself

Physical	Emotional	Intellectual

Medications Taken		
Drug	*Amount*	*Time(s)*

Things to Tell or Ask Doctor

	Exercise		

	Nutrition		
Breakfast	*Lunch*	*Supper*	*Snacks*

Daily Rating (1–10) Pain   Stiffness

Journal

	Exercise		

Nutrition			
Breakfast	*Lunch*	*Supper*	*Snacks*

Daily Rating (1–10) Pain _____ Stiffness _____

Journal

Exercise			

Nutrition			
Breakfast	*Lunch*	*Supper*	*Snacks*

Daily Rating (1–10) Pain _____ Stiffness _____

Journal

Date _____

What I Hope to Accomplish

Have To	Should Do	Want To

What I Will Do for Myself

Physical	Emotional	Intellectual

Medications Taken		
Drug	*Amount*	*Time(s)*

Things to Tell or Ask Doctor

Exercise			

Nutrition			
Breakfast	*Lunch*	*Supper*	*Snacks*

Daily Rating (1–10) Pain _____ Stiffness _____

Journal

Date

What I Hope to Accomplish

Have To	Should Do	Want To

What I Will Do for Myself

Physical	Emotional	Intellectual

Medications Taken		
Drug	Amount	Time(s)

Things to Tell or Ask Doctor

Exercise			

Nutrition

Breakfast	Lunch	Supper	Snacks

Daily Rating (1–10) Pain _____ Stiffness _____

Journal

Date

What I Hope to Accomplish

Have To	Should Do	Want To

What I Will Do for Myself

Physical	Emotional	Intellectual

Medications Taken		
Drug	*Amount*	*Time(s)*

Things to Tell or Ask Doctor

Exercise

Nutrition

Breakfast	Lunch	Supper	Snacks

Daily Rating (1–10) Pain _____ Stiffness _____

Journal

Date _____

What I Hope to Accomplish

Have To	Should Do	Want To

What I Will Do for Myself

Physical	Emotional	Intellectual

Medications Taken		
Drug	*Amount*	*Time(s)*

Things to Tell or Ask Doctor

	Exercise		

Nutrition			
Breakfast	*Lunch*	*Supper*	*Snacks*

Daily Rating (1–10) Pain   Stiffness

Journal

Date

What I Hope to Accomplish

Have To	Should Do	Want To

What I Will Do for Myself

Physical	Emotional	Intellectual

Medications Taken		
Drug	Amount	Time(s)

Things to Tell or Ask Doctor

	Exercise		

Nutrition			
Breakfast	*Lunch*	*Supper*	*Snacks*

Daily Rating (1–10) Pain _____ Stiffness _____

Journal

Date

What I Hope to Accomplish

Have To	Should Do	Want To

What I Will Do for Myself

Physical	Emotional	Intellectual

Medications Taken		
Drug	Amount	Time(s)

Things to Tell or Ask Doctor

256

		Exercise	

		Nutrition	
Breakfast	*Lunch*	*Supper*	*Snacks*

Daily Rating (1–10) Pain _____   Stiffness _____

Journal

Date _____

What I Hope to Accomplish

Have To	Should Do	Want To

What I Will Do for Myself

Physical	Emotional	Intellectual

Medications Taken		
Drug	*Amount*	*Time(s)*

Things to Tell or Ask Doctor

Exercise

Nutrition

Breakfast	Lunch	Supper	Snacks

Daily Rating (1-10) Pain   Stiffness

Journal

Date

What I Hope to Accomplish

Have To	Should Do	Want To

What I Will Do for Myself

Physical	Emotional	Intellectual

Medications Taken

Drug	Amount	Time(s)

Things to Tell or Ask Doctor

	Exercise		

	Nutrition		
Breakfast	*Lunch*	*Supper*	*Snacks*

Daily Rating (1–10) Pain   Stiffness _____

Journal

Index

Index

Index

Index

About the Author

Theodore W. Rooney received his B.A. degree from Miami University and earned a D.O. degree from Kirksville College of Osteopathic Medicine. Dr. Rooney currently serves as a Fellow Associate—Clinical Research in the Division of Rheumatology at the University of Iowa Hospital and Clinics in Iowa City, IA. He has been appointed as the Medical Director of the Mercy Hospital Arthritis Clinic in Des Moines upon completion of his clinical research. An experienced lecturer, Dr. Rooney has spoken on arthritis at medical society and hospital meetings throughout the country, and made many TV and radio appearances to discuss new developments in the treatment of arthritis. Dr. Rooney has published papers in the *Osteopathic Annals* and the *Iowa Medical Society Journal*, and is a member of the Iowa Chapter of the Arthritis Foundation, the American Rheumatism Association, and the American College of Physicians.

Patty Ryan Rooney received her B.S.E. degree in English from Northeast Missouri State University and has taught English at the secondary level. She is a published freelance writer and has written a book on early childhood and a children's book, both pending publication. The Rooneys and their three small daughters reside in Coralville, Iowa.